LONG ROAD
ROAD
to
ZAÏRE

GRAHAM TOULMIN

Ark House Press
arkhousepress.com

© 2022 Graham Toulmin

All rights reserved. Apart from any fair dealing for the purpose of study, research, criticism, or review, as permitted under the Copyright Act, no part may be reproduced by any process without written permission.

Unless otherwise stated, all Scriptures are taken from the New International Translation (Holy Bible. Copyright© 1996, 2004, 2007, 2013 by Tyndale House Foundation. Used by permission of Tyndale House Publishers Inc., Carol Stream, Illinois 60188. All rights reserved.)

Some names and identifying details have been changed to protect the privacy of individuals.

Cataloguing in Publication Data:
Title: Long Road to Zaïre
ISBN: 978-0-6452860-9-0 (pbk)
Subjects: Memoirs; Missions;
Other Authors/Contributors: Wendy Toulmin

Design by initiateagency.com

FOREWORD

Missionary farewell services are exciting, joyous, celebratory, and prayerful. The farewell for Graham and Wendy was no exception. Myrtle and I were privileged to be there. We had come to know Wendy and Graham – active, musical and inspirational – at All Souls Langham Place in London. Now, here in Sydney, we would never forget the sight of Wendy conducting the orchestra with her youngest child under one arm and the baton in the other … and all the while, huge crates of family luggage and dental equipment, that had been so amazingly collected and given through Graham's initiative, were being loaded for the challenges ahead of them.

Everyone was moved by their sheer courage and dedication, their daring for God, the sacrifices already made and the enormous ones ahead. They were surrounded by love and prayer.

Yet, the farewells and the years of training, struggling with Swahili and coping with four lively boys, could never truly prepare them for landing in the dust and dirt of Butembo. No wonder Graham can say at one point: 'Lectures cannot prepare you … you just feel wretched'.

This is a TIAII book. Tell It As It Is. It is a synthesising of the *Touligrams* (their early newsletters from the field), written firsthand … it has Aussie grit, christian grace, incredible sacrifice and dedication, honesty about the overwhelming challenges to be met and the wonderful Toulmin sense of humour.

As I started, the day's Bible reading was in Hebrews 12 and seemed so utterly appropriate: 'Let us run with perseverance the race marked out for us, fixing our eyes on Jesus'. They have done just that, amazing perseverance in spite of everything they have had to handle, only possible because they had their eyes fixed on Jesus. One lays down the book with awe, applause, enormous gratitude and with praise to the Lord who called and sustained them. And we hear afresh the challenge to our own lives: 'let **us** run with perseverance the race marked out for **us**, fixing **our** eyes on Jesus'.

Rt Rev Michael Baughen
Former Rector of All Souls Langham Place and Bishop of Chester

INTRODUCTION

I didn't want to write home about the shooting. Our parents were nervous enough about Wendy and I being in Zaïre in the first place. The fact that we had taken their four young grandchildren, aged two to eight years, to this remote location in central Africa, made it an even more emotionally charged issue.

From the perspective of many Australians in the 1980s, Zaïre was a largely unknown and forgotten part of the world – a distant and dangerous place. For our parents, there was no point writing up stories that would fuel the fires of ongoing anxiety.

Our bank manager in Springwood had summed up what many thought when I sold my dental practice in the lower Blue Mountains, west of Sydney, with the intention of going as a missionary dentist, with my family, to Zaïre. *'Toulmin'* he said, *'you've got rocks in your head!'*

Rocks or not, we had finally arrived in Zaïre. Our destination, after more than two and a half years' preparation, was in a lush mountainous region in the Province of North Kivu, at an altitude of around 5500 ft (1600 m) and 16 miles (26 km) north of the Equator. The climate was mild at that altitude and we set up home in a city called Butembo.

This was a bustling, sprawling, vibrant, colourful, and chaotic African town of 150,000. It was a fascinating but tough place to which I had brought my family. With all the preparation, we were still not ready for the surprises ahead.

LONGROADTOZAÏRE

The *shooting* story happened in our first year in Zaïre, but that story will have to wait. The question I want to address, looking back over half a lifetime, is the question that our bank manager raised, a question that some of our children, now adults and with children of their own, have jokingly raised: 'Mum and Dad, what were you thinking?'

This is the story of *why* and *how* Wendy and I embarked on our long road to Zaïre and our final arrival there, and I want to thank Wendy for not only travelling this road with me, but for editing my writing to create this book. I feel the story needs to be recorded, first as a family history and secondly as a CMS (Church Missionary Society) story, one of possibly thousands of stories that their missionaries could tell.

This story, our family's story, is just one of those many, and it began for me when I was growing up as a boy in Wollongong, a town south of Sydney, with an emergency trip to the dentist.

Graham Toulmin AM BDS (Syd) FICD
2022

For Wendy and our sons, Matthew, Michael, Stephen, and Jeremy.

THE ROAD BEGINS

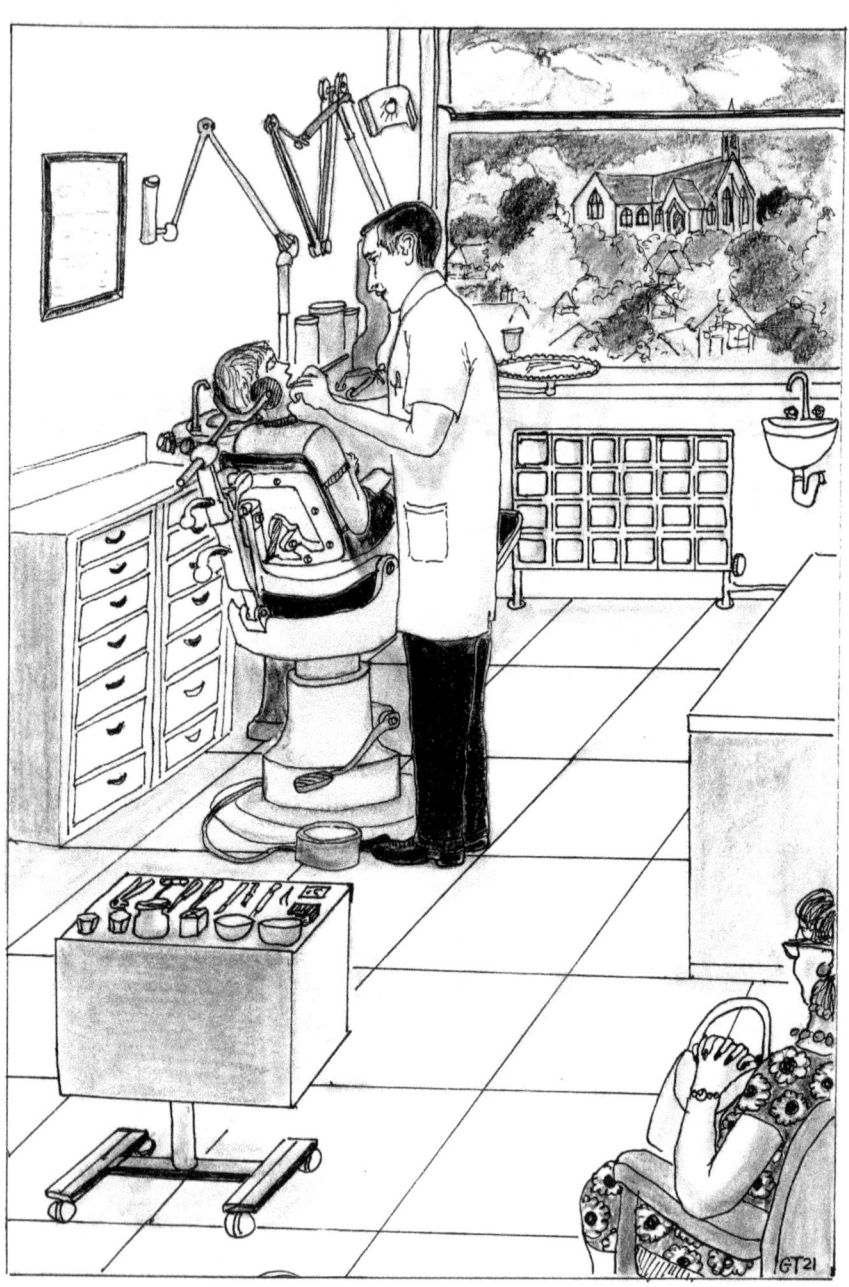

DENTIST IN THE CHAIR

The year was 1960. I was a 12-year-old boy with a smashed front tooth. I don't remember the day of the accident. It happened while I was playing the cornet.

I had always wanted to play the trumpet from the time I was old enough to listen to jazz, swing and brass bands on the radio in the early 1950s. At age six, my father made enquiries about lessons. He was told by his friend, Jack Tougher, the bandmaster of the Wollongong Steelworks Band, to wait until my permanent front teeth had come down into place.

At the age of nine, I began lessons on the cornet, the brass band equivalent of the trumpet. When I was ready, Mr Tougher invited me to join the band in the Third Cornet seat. This A grade brass band played various competitions, concerts, and marches in and around Wollongong and Sydney, to the north. Over the next seven years I would progress to the Solo Cornet seat.

It's a strange thing when you are playing a brass instrument like a cornet in a public setting, some people, thinking they are being funny, have a desire to bang the end of the trumpet when you have it to your lips. This is what happened to me, causing injury to my mouth and one of my front teeth. The lips healed quickly but the left central incisor didn't recover. Within weeks the tooth had 'died' and was turning black. I was on my way to the dentist.

Our family dentist was a tall, friendly man called Keith Gray. In the days before dentists were called 'Doctor', my family knew him as 'Mr Gray'. Located in Market Street, Wollongong, just behind the Keira Street shops and the town's Regent Theatre, Mr Gray's dental surgery looked out on the hill with the Anglican Cathedral on top. He had two treatment rooms, each with a dental chair of that era, very old-fashioned and quaint now, but modern then. My Mum or Dad, usually my Mum after she acquired her driving licence, would wait with me in the little waiting room, looking at old magazines and listening to the sounds coming out of the treatment rooms behind the door with the round glass panel. Sounds that weren't always encouraging.

The nurse, whose name was Barbara, who had worked for Mr Gray as long as we could remember, would call me from the waiting room. With my parent close by, I would enter one of these little treatment rooms, ominously called 'surgeries', and Barbara would get me seated. There was another chair for Mum or Dad to sit in. When I was comfortable, and before Mr Gray arrived, Barbara would drop a large tablet into a glass of water alongside the spittoon, which would fizz and turn the water pink and give it a nice taste.

With all the scary equipment to look at, it was no wonder most kids were terrified of going to the dentist. But Mr Gray and Barbara were always very patient, kind, and methodical – explaining what they were doing as they carried out treatment. As I had a sweet tooth and poor toothbrushing technique, I had spent many hours in Mr Gray's chairs in previous years, often having 'baby teeth' extracted under 'gas'.

Although I was usually a bit nervous at first sitting in his chair waiting for him to come, once he had arrived, he would have a bit of a chat and I started to feel at ease. If he had to do any treatment, drilling or extracting, he always placed numbing paste on the gum and then gave the needle slowly and painlessly. I found that it wasn't all that bad after all.

I came to accept having dental treatment as just part of growing up, and even found myself feeling as though I could fall asleep while being treated. Except on one occasion when I didn't have the numbing paste and the needle.

'This tooth is dead' Mr Gray informed my parents, 'so Graham won't need an injection.' He picked up the high-speed handpiece. Drilling a hole in the back of the tooth and finding the canal down the middle of the tooth that holds the nerve, he then introduced a 'K' file. The tooth had all the appearance of being 'dead'. He was not to know there were still *live* bits in there.

Peeling me off the ceiling was not easy. After giving me some local anaesthetic, the world became a much better place. Mr Gray apologised profusely. I settled back in the chair, the anaesthetic took effect, and the treatment began. *(I had just learnt, unknowingly, a valuable lesson for when I would be a dentist in the future.)* This 'root canal therapy' treatment meant several appointments looking up Mr Gray's nostrils – the age of masks had not arrived – but it was successful, and 60 years later I still have that tooth.

Despite this experience, I still liked Mr Gray and didn't fear my visits. I had no idea that the dental work I was having, and the kindness he showed would, in a strange way, encourage me to follow in his footsteps in years to come.

I also could not have imagined, at that age, that the hours of practising the cornet and developing the ability to play a brass instrument, would one day raise funds for clinics in Africa where I would one day work and teach.

Fast forward five years. It was the 'Careers Night' at Wollongong High School in my final year. I was wandering aimlessly around the school assembly hall and wondering which of the career representatives to talk with. I had no idea what I wanted to do except that I knew that I didn't want to be a builder like my father. I had done some 'work experience' with him during the holidays, unloading and stacking thousands of bricks, and had decided it wasn't for me. It meant working in the hot sun, getting sunburnt, doing hard physical labour unloading and stacking more and more of those bricks, digging trenches, mixing cement. I watched my father doing long hours during the day. On top of that, I saw

Dad doing long hours at night in the little home office, looking at plans and doing quotes for clients.

No, building was not for me. But what could I do?

'I have always liked drawing,' I thought to myself. 'Maybe I could do architecture? Maybe I could be a cartoonist?' On the musical side, I had competed in the New South Wales B-flat Cornet Championship that year and had won the Junior State Champion trophy playing Rossini's 'Una Voce'. 'Maybe a professional musician?' was another thought. Who knows? I had no firm ideas about my future career.

I saw the sign that said 'MEDICINE' and thought 'maybe that's a possibility?' ... but there were about fifty students around the doctor, and it was impossible to get near to hear what he was saying or to ask questions. There was another impediment to me doing medicine. I thought, at the immature age of 16, I couldn't handle the fact that your patients sometimes die, so I kept looking.

There was a sign saying 'DENTISTRY' with someone standing underneath and not one student. 'Dental patients generally don't die', I thought to myself. Also, I felt a bit sorry for him being on his own. I drifted past the crowd surrounding the doctor and went over to have a chat with the dentist.

I talked to Austen Jones for over an hour. He was an interesting bloke and he encouraged me to go back and talk to Keith Gray who was a friend of his. I did ... and Mr Gray invited me to come and watch him work during the school holidays. I did ... and I found that I *was* interested in dentistry.

Mr Gray became a mentor to me. After the initial visit to watch him work, he invited me to come to his surgery any day after school for a kind of informal work experience. He got me a Christmas holiday job with the dental technician next door, who introduced me to the world of prosthetics – making dentures or 'false teeth' as everyone called them.

When I sat for the Leaving Certificate later that year, my results were good enough for Dentistry. I didn't get a Commonwealth Scholarship, meaning we'd have to pay for the course, but Mum and Dad were excited I would be going to Sydney University. I was totally naïve about the costs of university. I had no idea what it would entail, what would happen at the end of the course, where I would work in the future and, the bottom line, I didn't appreciate how hard my Dad would have to work to pay for it. It was just an exciting possibility opening for me. I had no idea of the depressing and challenging times ahead.

UNIVERSITY BLUES

1966 The start of the academic year at Sydney University couldn't come quick enough. It was the first day of Orientation Week. I took the train from Wollongong, on my own, to enrol in the Faculty of Dentistry. I was almost 18. Straight out of school. 'University' was part of the rite of passage to oncoming adulthood.

I recall the feeling of awe and awkwardness as I walked up the sweeping entrance of Sydney University. The main campus is one of the most beautiful in the world. It was all so impressive. The sandstone buildings from another age, reminiscent of Oxford and Cambridge. The main administrative block ahead of me, the Great Hall on the right. In front of the main building, scores of colourful tents all advertising the various societies and sports that you could join. On all sides were manicured lawns covered in students, sitting, standing, debating, laughing. Men bearded, with long straggly hair, in T-shirts and jeans. Many dressed like hippies – a far cry from the high school uniform. The girls were dressed in skimpy miniskirts, jeans, and flowing kaftans.

Walking tentatively through an archway, I entered the Quadrangle and began searching for the place to enrol in the Dental Faculty. There were students sitting and lounging in groups on the inner lawns. Some deep in conversation, some sleeping in the sun. There was obvious freedom here. Everywhere and everything was impressive – the lecture theatres, the library, the coffee shops, the Student Union, the football fields, and cricket pitches; not to mention the Colleges dotted around the tree-filled campus. It was mind-boggling to a young man just arriving. I found the office and enrolled. I was now a university student.

Away from home for the first time, I needed accommodation and found it on the university campus. Wesley College was not a cheap place to board ($25 a week in 1966) but I convinced my parents that it was the place to be. Close to the lecture theatres and the time saved not having to travel, could be put to good use studying. They agreed and I moved into a whole different world.

First year Dentistry was on campus, the subjects being Physics, Chemistry, Biology, and a subject of your choice – I chose Psychology. With a great deal of nervousness, I explored campus and began attending lectures. What surprised me was nobody cared if you attended or not. You were treated as adults and made your own decisions. If you wanted to pass, you attended. If you wanted the social life, you went to Manning House and drank coffee or to the pubs nearby, the Whitehorse or the Governor Bourke, and 'had a few' with your new friends. If you wanted to do *really well*, you put your head down and didn't look up until the exams came, and hopefully, the credits, distinctions and high distinctions followed. But 'blood, sweat and tears' were needed, and I wasn't prepared for that.

I was restless, unsure of myself, away from home, needing friends, seeking guidance but getting none, wanting to fit in at the college and with my fellow students. My results at high school had come reasonably easily but university was a different thing. I was out of my depth and I was about to experience the harsh realities of the tertiary education world.

Looking back, I realise I was in no way mature enough for university, or living away from home, especially staying in a college like Wesley. Back then, there was the Fresher system. You came in as a first year and were immediately put in your place, the lowest rank possible. Lorded over by the senior students, if you fell out of favour, you became their 'slave' or were ostracised. I know this sounds somewhat antiquated, but this form of 'fresher-bashing' was there, and if you didn't fit in you suffered.

So, for an 18-year-old away from home … you fit in. You go to the pub and get used to drinking beer. I hated the taste of it at first, but persevered. Getting freshers drunk was extremely amusing to senior students but extremely unpleasant for the victim. I remember thinking, on such occasions, 'this is meant to be having a good time?!'

The problem with Wesley was the fun and the peer pressure. Social life took over and I found myself in local pubs and at the college snooker table when I should have been in my room and 'on the books'.

As the exams approached the end of first year, the social life and snooker lost its appeal. I began studying frantically but unfortunately it was too late to make up for lost time. I was about to receive a heavy dose of 'university blues'.

Christmas 1966, I tore open *The Sydney Morning Herald* and began scanning the University Results pages. I couldn't find my name. It must be here somewhere, I reassured myself. There was rising nauseating panic as the realisation hit me.

I had failed.

Only the successful students' names appeared in the paper. I couldn't believe it. I knew I hadn't done much work. I had never failed before and I was in shock.

My parents asked how I had gone. When I said my name was missing, my mother began crying and Dad became very quiet. Inwardly, no doubt, he was very disappointed and angry. He had worked hard to give me this chance at university, a chance he and Mum never had. 'This is not good' he said, a remarkable understatement, following up with 'so, what are you going to do now?'

After some days to process what it meant for him and me, he said he'd give me another chance.

SINKING FAST – TWO LIFELINES

1967 I re-enrolled at Sydney University but couldn't return to Wesley College. At Wesley, you forfeited your accommodation if you failed. I had to look for new 'digs' and found a place at Centennial Park. It was the Church of England's National Emergency Fund (CENEF) Hostel and *much* cheaper than Wesley.

My year at CENEF Hostel brought success. I did a lot more work and passed all subjects the first time. My parents were very happy and just quietly, so was I.

Looking back, I don't know what came over my parents when I passed that year, but somehow, I convinced them that I should move back to Wesley. This was a decision that we would all live to regret.

1968 Second Year Dentistry began and most of the lectures and practical sessions were again on campus. The subjects were Anatomy in the Medical School, which included dissections of cadavers, Physiology, Biochemistry, Histology and one dental subject at the Dental Hospital, just to whet our appetites for the career ahead.

The dental subject Prosthetics consisted of two parts – Denture Making and Dental Materials. At the time, I found Dental Materials one of the world's most boring subjects. It included knowing the composition of wax, plaster, and other dental products, with some metallurgy thrown in. I still don't know what 'eutectics' and 'peritectics' are to this day.

Sadly, with the move back to Wesley, the year began heading in the same direction. The same temptations raised their heads and began shouting at me. Dissections in the Anatomy Building and other practical sessions were often cut short so that a group of us could drink cappuccinos and socialise in Manning House, on the top floor. The Wesley social life also took over again and I improved my snooker. I must have been blind not to see what was happening.

However, I did spend a bit more time in my room studying and when the results appeared in *The Sydney Morning Herald* in December, I hadn't passed, but I hadn't failed either. My name was there – but I had only passed two and a half subjects out of five. I therefore needed to re-sit three exams: Histology, Physiology … and Dental Materials which, as I said above, was only half a subject.

When the deferred exams came round, in early 1969, I made a fateful decision. I can see now, with the benefit of hindsight, it was a really dumb decision, but I fell headlong into the trap … I took a gamble on what to study for the Dental Materials exam. I convinced myself the exam would cover the subject matter that wasn't covered in the first exam I had failed. That seemed reasonable, I thought. So, I put all my effort into studying the areas of the course missing from the first paper.

The medical exams came, and I sailed through.

The day of Dental Materials arrived. I entered the exam room, took my seat at one of the portable wooden desks spread throughout the room and looked at the exam paper, face down in front of me.

The invigilator said, 'You may now turn over the paper and begin.'

I turned the paper. 'Oh no!'

The blood drained from my face. I felt sick. It was *exactly* the same paper as the first time. At that moment, I knew I was gone. I sat there in a catatonic state, castigating myself, again and again. 'You are an *idiot!*' was the only thought in my head, going round and round. I tried to pull myself together and made a futile attempt at all questions, but it was obvious, even to me, that I didn't know the work.

The Sydney Morning Herald published the results the following week. My name was not there. If ever there was a time in my life when I thought about the possibility of ending it, it was that morning holding the newspaper.

My father had worked long and hard to put me through three years of university, with nothing to show for it. I had failed twice now. The money Dad and Mum had invested in my future career, who knows how much, had just gone down the drain. Two failures out of three years meant I couldn't continue in dentistry so that was that. 'I'm out of university' was the depressing thought that hit me 'and I'll have to start looking for a job of some kind.'

Mum again was crying. Dad, a quiet man at the best of times, didn't get angry. He just looked at me and said 'Well … you've really blown it this time, son.'

1969 It was the week before university started again. My father called me aside and spoke softly to me: 'You don't deserve it … (I held my breath) … but I am going to give you another chance.' 'Tomorrow', he went on, 'we are going up to Sydney to see the Dean of Dentistry, Professor Noel Martin. I've made an appointment. We'll see what he has to say.' In the background, Mum tried to smile to encourage me. I nodded to Dad, thankful for what he had done, and went back to my bedroom deep in thought.

The journey to Sydney the next day was quiet. We found a parking spot near the Dental Hospital situated alongside Central Railway and entered the building. We took the lift to the sixth floor and with a great deal of trepidation, entered the Dean's office. His secretary greeted us and asked us to sit and wait. The inner door opened, and Professor Martin beckoned us in. 'Have a seat' he said gently. 'What can I do for you?' he continued. Dad explained the situation, but the Dean knew full well why we were there.

He asked me some questions and then swung his chair around and looked out of the window, past the trains arriving and departing, deep in thought. He turned back to us and addressed me sternly. 'This is what we are going to do. You can repeat the year (my heart leapt, Mum sobbed, Dad blew his nose silently), but you have to do all the subjects again. Knuckle down, young man, and do some work. You have the capacity. Let's now see some decent results.' And with that, he stood. The interview was over. He showed us to the door. 'You had better go and enrol' he added, as he turned and closed the door, leaving us with his secretary who smiled knowingly. We headed for the lifts.

'I don't believe it' I thought to myself. 'Oh darling, that is so wonderful!' Mum gushed. Dad said nothing, just smiled a little, put his hand on my shoulder and with the other hand pushed the button for the ground floor.

I re-enrolled, but the problem of accommodation had to be faced. As I wandered round the campus, I met John Mebberson. John had been a year ahead of me at Wollongong High School and we got talking about the accommodation problem.

'Mate,' he said, 'I just found the perfect place. Cheap as chips. Only $8 a week for full board.'

'*Really*! $8 a week. Where?'

'Enfield, near Strathfield. On the Hume Highway. You've got a Yamaha 80 motorbike. It's about 20 minutes on that. You should come and have a look. They've got a few vacant rooms.'

He paused. 'But I've got to tell you this. It's a college where they train ministers for the Methodist Church. But I've found they're not bad blokes, and they don't try to stuff their religion down your throat. It's pretty good actually and the cost of the accommodation – mate, you can't get full board any cheaper anywhere. The rooms are large, the food's not bad and you don't have to be religious to get a room.'

I made enquiries, talked to Mum and Dad, and within a few days, just before lectures started, I moved into Leigh College as one of the few non-theological boarding students.

MATE, I NEED A HAND WITH YOUR BAND

Leigh College was the sort of place where 'religion' was talked about all the time. The 'minister types' were always having 'brews', usually a big pot of coffee in one of the student's rooms or the common room, and there you would find them after lectures, chatting or arguing about the Sermon on the Mount, the meaning of life and who won the 'footy' on the weekend.

However, the students were very friendly and welcoming to outsiders like 'Mebs' and me, and there was none of the fresher-bashing that I had experienced at Wesley.

Because it was a Methodist College, 'drinking' was frowned upon, so no alcohol was allowed, but the coffee breaks were plentiful. They often asked me in for a 'brew' and if the topic got around to something awkward, I would find an excuse to leave and return to my room, ostensibly for some study.

One of the characters amongst the students was George Davies, the Deputy Senior Student. George was one of the first people who welcomed me to the college. He was larger than life, a folk musician who sang and played guitar. He was a born entertainer and entrepreneur and just a little bit eccentric. He was in his final year of studying to become a Methodist minister. He loved people and performing and so he was often found organising one event or another. Sometimes they were folk nights, sometimes jazz nights and some of these events were held in the cobwebby basement of the college. Lots of atmosphere.

Over the months, 'Mebs' and I became quite friendly with George and each night, around 10pm, we'd visit his room to find him at his desk, either studying or sound asleep with his head on his books. We'd wake him up and ask if he wanted a hamburger from the local cafe before it shut. *(This was before McDonalds was heard of in Australia.)*

'Yeah … yeah … I've got a big essay to write. I need to do an all-nighter! Can you get me a hamburger with bacon and egg? Thanks guys, here's some money.'

We'd return with the hamburgers and call into his room and often he would be sound asleep again. He was very hard to wake up, so we would leave the hamburger beside his head. There were many days he ate it for breakfast.

1969 was the folk era. Bob Dylan and Peter Paul and Mary were at the top of the hit parade. Coffee shops were the 'in' places to hear live music. They had sprung up everywhere. Everyone was getting a guitar, learning a few chords, and offering to sing on the 'open mike' that these coffee shops offered most Friday and Saturday nights. So, it was no surprise when George, as a Christian musician, opened an outreach coffee shop which he called *Snoopy's Jazz and Folk Cellar* in the Guildford Methodist Church Hall where he had been assigned as the student minister. It took place on the first Friday of the month.

On the morning of the first Friday in August 1969, George came to me in a sort of laid-back panic.

'Hey Touls, what are you and your band mates doing tonight?'

'I dunno, George. Why?'

'I've got a problem. The folk singers who are supposed to be singing tonight at Snoopy's have let me down. Mate, I'm in trouble. Can your guys come and play? What do you reckon?'

'I dunno, George, I'm seeing them at Uni today. What's the deal? You realise we're not a band as such, we're just a bunch of guys who play to amuse ourselves. This would be our first-ever gig.'

'That's fine. I'm desperate. Tell them they need to be at Snoopy's at seven to set up and start playing at seven-thirty while all the young kids are coming in. You know, bit of ambience. And don't worry, you'll get paid. How does $15 for the five of you sound? That's the best we can do,

Touls. You know … it's a church coffee shop and people don't pay to get in, just for the coffees. Can you do it, mate? You'll really help me out!'

'I'll see what I can do, George.'

And with that I headed off on my motorbike to lectures.

Our band didn't have a name. As I said, we were just a bunch of blokes that got together to play music for fun. These practices took place in one of the common rooms at Wesley College that had a piano. The college was central for all the band members, and Keith Roberts, our pianist and a law student, was a Wesley boarder who had passed all his exams, so we had permission to use the room. Keith also had the gift to be able to play anything you named without music. Steve Creak (doing Engineering) played trombone while John Mebberson, (Geology) my old mate, was on bass. Steve Anderson, (also an Engineering student) played drums and I was on trumpet. I contacted the guys and surprisingly, everyone could do the gig.

We arrived at the church hall and discussed what we should call our band for the night. There were some catchy band names around the university campus such as 'The Rubber Band', and Keith knew a band at Armidale University called 'Adams Zapple Corps', a name which I thought was pretty cool at the time and still do. We tossed various ideas around and decided for the night we would be 'Brass Razoo', which was about what they were paying us.

We did the gig, and, to our amazement, they loved us. We disappeared during the Christian talk George gave towards the end of the night and drank beers out the back, even though we knew Methodists were teetotal and the church leaders probably wouldn't have approved. For that first gig, we pocketed $3 each, (worth every penny) and headed home rather satisfied.

George was sufficiently impressed that he asked us to be the resident band each month. Guest singers would arrive and do their spot while we 'topped and tailed' the night. Nice. None of the band members were what we called 'religious' but that didn't seem to matter to George. He liked us and we liked him and so he tolerated us. But something was about to happen that would change my thinking in ways I never imagined.

MEETING WENDY

It was Friday the third of October 1969 I saw the girl I was going to marry.

I didn't know that at the time. I just thought she was attractive and wondered how I might be introduced. Wendy and her sister were the guest singers that night – two girls, introduced by MC George, as 'Julie and Wendy, the Stirling Sisters' – with a mixed repertoire of songs, some folksy, some 'religious', some funny. The one that still sticks in my mind was 'Three Little Fishies' which I thought was seriously cute. I was hooked on the singer on the right.

But what to do? How do I get to know this girl? And then, never short of ideas, I had a great one!

I managed to persuade George it would be good, chivalrous even, for Steve the Drummer and me to drive these two young girls home. 'No, no, no!' I protested. 'It's not out of our way' (only a 30 km detour).

And so, it was decided.

On the way, there was much talking and laughing. They were good company. When we arrived, I managed to stall Wendy's departure for a minute or two and, gathering all my courage, asked if she would join me and the band for a gig the following Friday night.

'It's the Vet. Science Informal Ball', I explained eagerly, 'at the Round House at New South Wales University. There are two bands playing so when the other band is playing, we can dance. It should be a great night.'

'You'll come? Great! I'll pick you up early. We need to get the gear there and set up.'

The day arrived. I was nervous about 'the first date' but doubly so because I was running an hour and a half late!

The traffic on Beecroft Road that Friday evening was thick, and I was pushing the Austin Somerset hard trying to get through the congestion while looking for the turn-off to Lyon Road.

'Strike, I'm late. Hope she doesn't mind.' I had a good excuse, I thought. I had to pick up the drum kit and the bass amp. It took longer with the traffic. 'Now where is Lyon Road?' Cheltenham was unfamiliar territory to me.

'Ah, there it is!' I flung the car through a hole in the traffic flow coming round an almost blind corner. 'The Crescent must be ahead.' I had memorised the pages of the *Gregory's Street Directory* and figured out her house must be to the right at the T intersection. I careered round the corner into *The Crescent* and there, right in front of me, was a middle-aged man in a suit with a briefcase walking home from the train. At the speed I was going it was just a momentary glance. I braked quickly. The man in a suit with a briefcase was able to scuttle to safety into a roadside 'ditch'.

'Oops, sorry,' I mouthed to myself, as I left the startled man in my wake. 'I'm running a bit late', I added, to no one in particular.

I was more pre-occupied with getting to Wendy's house and making my apologies.

I steered the Austin down the hill alongside the railway line, through a dip, accelerated up the other side, braking as I came over the rise.

'Number 100 must be here somewhere.' 'Ah, there it is.' I swung the car into the driveway. Neatly mown grass. Well-kept garden. Nice flowers. Bit nervous. Quite a bit nervous.

I stopped the car by the front door causing the drums to take up a different position in the back. I hopped out of the car and pressed the doorbell. Wendy's mother appeared at the door. I introduced myself politely.

'Hello Mrs Stirling. I'm … er, Graham Toulmin. It's very nice to meet you.' 'Er … yes, I'm a second-year dental student. Er … yes Sydney University. Er … yes I'll try to get Wendy home early, but the gig is at the University of New South Wales and we probably won't get back before 1am.'

'Sorry I'm late, ... er, bit of a problem picking up some gear for the gig.'

'Yes, I will drive carefully.' 'Yes, I'll look after your daughter.'

'Er ... is Wendy ready?' Considering I was so late, it was unlikely she would not have been ready. At that moment, Wendy appeared.

'Hi ... um, I brought some flowers.' She smiled and thanked me. I think she's impressed.

Her mother took the flowers (I think she was impressed too).

I open the car door (my Mum and Dad taught me to do that).

I was still a bit embarrassed and blurted out 'Er, sorry I'm late'.

I began reversing out.

At that moment, Wendy looked over her shoulder and exclaimed 'Oh, here's Dad.'

I turned and looked down the driveway.

A terrible nauseating feeling rushed through my body, not unlike the feeling in the Dental Materials exam. Coming towards my side of the car in the driveway was a somewhat familiar neatly dressed businessman in a suit with a briefcase.

'Oh no!' I thought.

The man in the suit with the briefcase, whom I had just forced into the gutter, walked up my side of the car. I wound down my window and prepared for the worst. He was polite but quite stern and I received a little lecture about looking after his daughter ('Yes Sir') and driving more calmly ('Yes Sir') and being home early ('Yes Sir – oh, it doesn't finish till after midnight, but Yes Sir').

That was *so* embarrassing, I was thinking as I reversed out, and drove up the hill. My embarrassment only grew worse as I was forced to ask Wendy the question I had been dreading to ask.

'Um...er...have you got any money? I'm a bit broke until I get paid tonight. I don't have money for the Harbour Bridge toll.'

Wendy fumbled in her purse and produced 10 cents, the toll in 1969. *(I only found out years later that the 10-cent coin was for the phone call the parents hoped she wouldn't have to make: 'Help. Come and get me!')*

Strangely enough Wendy continued to go out with me to various gigs with our band and other exciting venues like the *Rocks Push* where you could hear excellent jazz from the up-and-coming band 'Galapagos Duck' *and* eat a large bowl of spaghetti bolognese for just 17 cents. Yes really, 17 cents. Drinks, on the other hand, were expensive but the cheap food and the great jazz lured many in. It was a pity that sometime later it burnt down. *The Basement* took over as the predominant jazz venue in Sydney.

From my point of view, as a second-year dental student, her family home became like a 'home away from home' for me and most Saturday nights I found myself enjoying Mrs Stirling's baked dinners. A full timetable during the week meant making the most of the weekends and so, to be able to see Wendy on Sunday as well, I had to start going to church.

I was not entirely thrilled with this development.

SACRIFICES YOU HAVE TO MAKE

I had come from what I would have called, at that time, a 'semi-religious' family. My mother was an irregular church attender at Holy Trinity Anglican Church, Mount Ousley. My father was a member of the Masonic Lodge and a fine man, but he never went near a church. I never found out why. We didn't talk about stuff like that.

My older stepbrother, my younger sister and I had been taken to the Anglican Sunday School from an early age by my mother. At age nine, I was very excited to become 3rd cornet in the brass band. The band rehearsals were on Tuesday night and Sunday morning. Both these practice times required a degree of sacrifice for a nine-year-old.

The first sacrifice involved band practice on Tuesday nights. This meant missing a new TV show all the kids were talking about. It was called 'The Flintstones'.

The second 'sacrifice' involved Sunday School. This didn't bother me all that much as I wasn't so keen on church or Sunday School.

But my maternal grandmother, Ellen Fisher, took the whole thing very seriously. Known affectionately as 'Manma' because an earlier grandchild couldn't say 'Grandma', she was what I would have called 'religious' back then, but she would always say 'No! I'm not religious. I'm a Christian'.

It was in her home in Warrawong when I was about five or six that I first set eyes on an African person. This man had been speaking at the

Anglican Church where Manma played the organ. She had invited him home to have lunch with her family. I sat opposite him and marvelled at how very black his skin was, how white his teeth, how very deep and loud his voice, and how very colourful his clothes. *(I did not realise at the time that thirty-something years later many people like this visitor would be some of my dearest friends.)*

I learnt a lot of things sitting in church as a young boy. Some of them important and others frowned upon, like letting off a cap gun during the sermon ...

At 15, I went to the youth fellowship at church. I listened to the Christian talks and was interested a little, but I was more interested in the social life with kids of the same age: Anne, Olga, Sydney, Brett, Don, and others. *(Not many years later, Don was killed fighting in the Vietnam War.)*

In my late teens, I was confirmed by the local Anglican Bishop. It was a rite of passage, something every young church member did. I had learned all the questions and answers from the Anglican Catechism and when I took the vows, I was sincere, I believed it all, I just wasn't committed. I was 'religious', to a degree, but I wasn't a 'Christian'.

In Wesley College it definitely was not cool to be 'Christian' or even mildly 'religious'. There were a few seriously religious guys in the college, who took part in the college chapel services, but the vast majority of College students attended because it was obligatory – I took the majority view, it was easier to fit in.

The trips back home to Wollongong became fewer and fewer, with less and less opportunities to get to Friday Fellowship or Sunday Night Youth Services. I fell away from church involvement quietly. It wasn't noticeable.

Now here I was, four years after my 'Confirmation', sitting in the third pew from the front on the left-hand side of Epping Presbyterian Church. Another sacrifice, except Wendy was sitting next to me and the Minister, Peter Boase, was a jovial, bald-headed and bouncing preacher who was pretty interesting, though I didn't tell Wendy that.

During that year I actually did some work in the week and was successful in my second attempt at Second Year. I shared the very exciting news with my parents. There it was in the *Sydney Morning Herald* for all to see. They were overjoyed. Wendy was next to hear – she and her parents were also very happy.

I was looking forward to beginning the clinical years of the dental course and ... gulp ... treating my first real patient.

FIRST PATIENTS

1970 I had finally made it! The 'Clinical Years'.
Third Year began, and from the start, they worked us hard. Unlike the first two years on the university campus, we were now full time at the Dental Hospital, 8am till 5pm. It felt like we were now on the road to becoming dentists.

The Sydney Dental Hospital was, and still is, a strange wedge-shaped building that you can't miss, standing eight stories tall alongside Central Railway. At the time I was a student it was painted pink. We, the dental students, spent our time that year going from the basement, where we changed into our dental coats, to the first floor to learn how to extract teeth, to the third floor for the denture-making laboratory, to the fifth floor for operative dental work, fillings and crowns. The sixth floor was the lecture theatre (and also the Dean's office which I remembered all too well). The eighth floor had a cafeteria where I remember enjoying many a crusty ham roll and cup of tea.

From Leigh College, it was easier and safer to catch a train from Strathfield Station than to take the motorbike. Most days I walked to the train with two dental mates called John. John Cannon and John Symond. The second John left dentistry and, down the track a bit, started a business called 'Aussie Home Loans' and never looked back. The first John and I continued with dentistry. I made good friends in that year of dentistry as we shared the 'horror stories' of working on our first patients.

Working on real patients was seriously nerve-wracking. At this stage we weren't allowed to give injections, but we could do simple fillings on patients.

My first patient was a 15-year-old red-headed girl carrying a wicker basket. She came into the clinic quite nervous. (I don't blame her!) She had no idea she was my first patient *ever*! I was more nervous than she was.

I greeted her confidently (always look as though you know what you are doing) and took her to one of the thirty or so upright, pump-up, pale yellow, now very old-fashioned, dental chairs that stood in three neat rows in the clinic looking out into Chalmers Street. I don't remember her name, but I do remember what I did to her.

I had the chair between Paul Tobin and Michael Urwand. Positioned alongside was my blue 'operative kit' which I was about to use for the first time. I was very proud of this little blue box with its many drawers filled with instruments and dental materials. 'I have really arrived as a dental student', I often thought as I carried it proudly in the lift from the basement to the fifth floor.

The slow-speed drill hung alongside the dental chair like the denuded wing of a pterodactyl. The drill had a foot pedal to drive it and the bur (drill bit) was turned by a cord that rotated along the upper and lower arms of the articulated 'wing'.

It was very important to learn to co-ordinate your foot pedal with the hand piece while working in the patient's mouth. That is to say, you had to start pushing the foot pedal with your right foot *after* you had carefully placed the low-speed drill in the patient's mouth and positioned it above the tooth you intended to drill.

'Be very careful!' was the order of each day in the clinic because you didn't want to cause the patient an injury – a cut lip, a lacerated tongue or worse.

When you had finished drilling, you took your foot off the foot pedal (being careful that you didn't drill too long with the 'slow-speed' because even a slow-moving drill can cause 'heat friction' which can damage the nerve). The bur stopped rotating, and you withdrew the drill and the bur from the mouth, again without causing injury.

FIRST PATIENTS

We were one of the first groups of students in the clinic to use the 'high-speed' drill, run on compressed air. This drill made cutting through the very hard layer of enamel so much simpler and quicker than the old slow-speed, head-rattling grinder. But with the speed of the high-speed you needed a water spray to cool the tooth otherwise you fried the dental nerve hidden inside the tooth.

The basic idea for restorative dentistry back then was to save the tooth by removing the decay. The next step was placing an insulating lining to protect the nerve hidden within. Then the final filling on top. There were all sorts of rules about cavity design and what to do if the decay was really deep and close to the nerve, but we were starting on simple cavities with shallow decay, so we couldn't do too much damage. To pass the year successfully we had to complete a set number of 'silver' fillings (amalgams) in the back teeth and tooth-coloured fillings (firstly silicates and then the newly introduced composite resin) in the front teeth.

The upper teeth are the hardest to restore for a beginner as you have to work upside down, and back to front, in a dental mirror. This takes a bit of time to get used to. With lower teeth, you are looking directly at what you are doing.

On the patient record card the red-headed girl presented to me, the filling required, the one to begin my dental career, was a small cavity in an *upper* premolar tooth.

All our student group had practised on 'phantom heads', (simulated upper and lower jaws that could be attached to a dental chair), before we got to real patients; but we all had a long way to go before using a dental mirror in the mouth became second nature.

I couldn't put it off any longer. It was time to start.

She was sitting in the chair with all this fearsome equipment dangling around her, fiddling with a tissue. Well, actually … she was tearing it to shreds.

I smiled reassuringly at her, greeted her, and began explaining as I had been taught:

'Today we are going to do a little filling on this tooth up here on the right-hand side.'

She reaches for another tissue from the box on her lap.

'It's only small so you won't need anaesthetic.' (When was the last time I heard something like that?)

Now she is tearing up the second tissue.

I pump up the chair and press the lever so the chair leans back. I pick up the mirror and have a good look at the tooth in question.

'Hmmm' I say knowingly.

I pick up the high-speed drill and look back in the mirror. I place the drill with the tiny diamond bur inside the mouth and find the tooth I am supposed to be drilling.

Where is that tooth? Oh, there it is! (The opposite direction to where I was going.)

I do a little practice just above the tooth, imagining that I am drilling – like a golfer practising his swing. I am doing this while looking in the mirror. When I want the drill to go right, it goes left. When I want it to go up, it goes down.

Try again. Upside down. Back to front.

My brain says, 'Let me get this straight. If I want the drill to go left, I go right in the mirror. If I want to go up, I go down. This is not easy. Have another go. Left is right, up is down. I'm sure I'll get the hang of it soon.'

'Why did I choose dentistry' is a recurring thought, that I push out of the way.

And I haven't even begun to drill yet.

I've got to start sometime; I can't just keep *pretending* I'm drilling this tooth.

I press the foot pedal.

The diamond bur in the high-speed drill in my hand begins to rotate.

At nearly 200,000 revolutions per minute.

'Whoaaaaa! That's fast.'

As soon as the bur begins to spin, the water spray comes on.

Now I can't see a thing. The tooth has disappeared. A torrent of water swamps the tooth and my mirror. I wipe the mirror on the bib and start again. The same thing happens.

FIRST PATIENTS

'How in heaven's name, do *real* dentists drill upper teeth, looking in a mirror that is covered in a constant waterfall? This is a nightmare!'

After I have had several attempts at starting, with water going everywhere, I realise the patient is about to drown. Her mouth is full, and she is making gurgling noises.

'Er … have a little spit', I say calmly.

She spits a large volume of high-speed-drill water into the spittoon. She is not enjoying this. I am not enjoying this. I reach for the saliva ejector, the life-saving gadget that we call 'the little sucker'.

'We'll try this', I say, with as much feigned confidence as I can muster and place it in the floor of her mouth. Loud slurping noises emanate from her oral cavity.

'Ah, that's better', I mumble, and pick up the high speed again.

I continue drilling. Bit by bit. Slowly. Tentatively. Without anaesthetic. Wiping water constantly off the mirror so I can see. It's only a shallow cavity, but is it hurting. I wonder.

The red-headed girl sinks lower in the chair.

The tiny cavity I had to cut (which now would take me under a minute) is still not finished after two hours.

The Professor decides to go for afternoon tea and a senior lecturer takes over.

'This girl needs anaesthetic', he observes immediately and goes to prepare the syringe. The girl has sunk quite low in the chair compared to when she came in at 2pm. Out of the corner of my eye, I notice her wicker basket is a little in the way for the senior lecturer *and* myself to both be at the chairside. I push it under the foot part of the pumped-up chair. It fits perfectly.

The senior lecturer returns and gives the anaesthetic. The girl relieved, relaxes and I finish that little filling close to 5pm. My self-confidence is shot to pieces with the time taken, and the suffering I have caused her. She looks totally exhausted after three hours in the chair and I prepare to let her go.

I have forgotten the wicker basket under the foot part of the chair. I press the lever to lower the chair. The chair descends rapidly and crushes the wicker basket.

I quickly pump up the chair, and with a reddening face, extract the crumpled basket.

'Same time next week?' I ask, smiling lamely.

She looks close to tears, nods, and heads for the door.

I pack up my operative kit and head for the basement to share the story with the others who have also just finished their first patient.

Learning to be a dentist is not easy.

Later that week, my second patient. A 12-year-old boy who didn't want *anyone* working in his mouth. His plan to avoid the inevitable was to rinse out as often as possible.

I still haven't got my foot-hand coordination quite working together at this early stage of my operative career. As I start to take the slow-speed drill out of the boy's mouth, I still have my foot on the foot pedal. The drill leaves the boy's mouth but the large round bur in the drill is still rotating at top speed. The boy heads for the spittoon and as he moves his head forward, the still-rotating large round bur catches his hair as it moves past and gets tangled. The bur grinds to a halt in his profusion of black hair. The boy grabs his head and is yelling 'Oh m' head. Oh m' hair!' As I'm leaning over him, I see the Professor coming down the line of chairs towards us. We were all scared of this Professor.

'Shhh! Be quiet', I pleaded, in a hushed voice.

I pulled the bur out of his hair and hung the handpiece back up in the holder.

The Professor passed us on his way to a student with his hand up. As he went past, I suddenly noticed a large tuft of black hair matted around the bur.

Fortunately, the Professor didn't.

THE ULTIMATUM AND THE PIZZA HUT

I was really growing to like Wendy and her family. I even started to think 'could this be the one?' And then it happened.
It was late March approaching my 22nd birthday. We were in church, third pew from the front, on the left close to the organ. Peter Boase had just closed the service in the way he always did, with the usual enthusiasm:

> *Go forth into the world in peace.*
> *Be of good courage.*
> *Hold fast that which is good.*
> *Render to no one evil for evil.*
> *Strengthen the fainthearted.*
> *Support the weak.*
> *Help the afflicted.*
> *Honour all people.*
> *Love and serve the Lord,*
> *rejoicing in the power of the Holy Spirit;*
> *and the blessing of God Almighty,*
> *Father, Son and Holy Spirit,*
> *be among you and remain with you always. Amen.*

I stood to go. Wendy stayed seated, deep in thought. I sat back down.

'You OK?' I asked concerned.

She didn't answer right away.

She was looking down at the floor, as though she was sick or depressed, but Wendy wasn't the kind of girl I had ever seen depressed.

'Is something wrong?' I asked.

'I can't go out with you anymore.'

The words stunned me. We hadn't had a fight or a disagreement.

'What is going on here?' I thought in a kind of panic. 'What do you mean?'

A long pause.

'I'm sorry, but I can't go out with you anymore.'

This didn't make sense.

'Why?' I asked plaintively. I wanted to know why.

'Well ... I am a Christian and you aren't, and we're going in different directions.'

'What? ... You're kidding me, right?'

'I'm sorry' were her final words.

I didn't know what to do. I was shocked. I was angry. I was dumb founded. I stood up, my face hot and flushed, my heart beating rapidly. I turned and moved out of the pew and looked back. Wendy stayed looking down. I headed for the door.

On the drive home, my mind was in turmoil.

'I never saw this coming' I told myself. How can this be? ... What's going on ...? ... How ridiculous! ... 'We're heading in different directions ... she said' ...

I was still talking to myself, running the scene over and over in my mind, as I crossed the Ryde Bridge heading for Enfield on Concord Road.

'Wait a minute. I know what she means!'

The light was dawning, 'Yes! ... I know what she means.'

Memories of Sunday School came flooding back. 'Surely she doesn't mean that?' 'Heaven and Hell! ... No! That's ridiculous! Who believes that these days?'

I started to get angry. 'Where's a Christian I can punch?' I thought, as I returned to my room in the training college for keen Christians. I wasn't serious, but the thought did go through my head.

THE ULTIMATUM AND THE PIZZA HUT

'Everything was going so well' I thought, as I stormed up the steps to the first floor.

'Hey Touls, how's it going mate?' Rob Forsyth, one of the first-year theological students greeted me cheerfully as he walked along the corridor.

'I hate cheerful Christians' I thought to myself.

'Not good' I replied angrily and opened the door to my room.

'Hey mate ... what's going on?' Forsyth followed me in.

'You wouldn't believe it. I'm going to bed. Sorry. I'll see you in the morning.'

The day after the ultimatum, I was at breakfast. Forsyth came and sat beside me.

'You OK?' he asked.

'Not really' I replied.

'You want to talk about it?'

I did, but not at breakfast, with lots of other students sitting around.

'Maybe later' I added, as I packed up my dishes and put them in the servery for Mrs Rhodes and Mrs Ames to deal with.

'Sorry, I've got an 8am lecture ... Bacteriology ... I'll see you tonight' and I turned to go.

It was a miserable day at Uni. When I returned to college, it was nearly dinner time and I slumped down at the table, deep in despair. My dilemma was obvious – I was wanting to keep going out with a girl, who I thought just might be the one I would like to marry, and it seemed she felt the same, but ... and this was the frustrating *but* ... she just happens to be a Christian, and she won't go out with me because I'm *not*.

'What if,' I reasoned, 'what if I could disprove Christianity? She could then go out with me again!' I was grasping at straws. I didn't know what to do and this seemed like a reasonable solution. 'Yes, that's it, I'll disprove Christianity,' I determined.

'Hey Touls, how was your day?' The cheery voice of Forsyth.

'Rubbish' I replied, or words to that effect.

'Mate, we need to talk. I have to do some work on an assignment straight after dinner, but what about we go for a pizza around 10pm?'

'10-ish, OK?' and he was off to his room.

I moped around till 10, couldn't study so watched some TV, killing time.

Just after 10, Forsyth appeared in the lounge room. I was the only one there.

'What about a large Supreme and a couple of beers?' he said.

'I thought Methodist students don't drink,' I replied with a smile.

'I'm maybe not a convinced Methodist' he grinned.

(In 1970, Pizza Hut opened its first franchise in Australia in Belfield, about 2 km from Leigh College. That was the place to go for a late-night snack and a beer. In those days, pubs closed at 10pm which fifty years later seems quite strange.)

Seated in the booth with a large Supreme and two beers, I told him the story and I began asking questions. At midnight, as the Pizza Hut was closing, we headed home. There were to be many more nights sitting in those booths discussing and arguing. My six-month battle with the Christian faith had begun. I had so many questions that I thought would beat Forsyth down.

'OK, Rob, if there is a God, why do people suffer? Why did my mate get killed in Vietnam? Why are there starving children if God is a God of love, as you say? You Christians are so arrogant, how can you say that Jesus is the only way to God, eh? What about all the other religions? Maybe he didn't die at all, maybe he just fainted, and in the tomb just revived? Maybe they made the whole thing up about him coming back from the dead. I mean to say … do you seriously believe that sort of Sunday School stuff?'

Rob was studying philosophy as part of his course and he had a gift – he was a natural debater. Every hard question I served across the net, he smashed back. Every ferocious delivery I bowled at him, he played with a straight bat and always with a joke. He never got sick of me asking question after question, but he kept on coming back to the same position.

Looking back over 50 years, I have tried to re-create snippets of the conversations I had with Rob, who later went on to study at *Moore College* and ended up as the Anglican Bishop of South Sydney. The bottom line was, 'Is the whole thing true or not?'

His defence of Christianity went something like this …

THE ULTIMATUM AND THE PIZZA HUT

'Touls, old mate,' he would say, looking me in the eye with a smile, 'if you want to disprove Christianity, you will have to disprove the resurrection of Jesus. It's as simple as that.'

'Paul, you know, the Apostle Paul. The one who wrote all those letters in the New Testament, well, that Paul was a total sceptic. He thought Christians were totally wrong. He persecuted Christians and stood by while the religious leaders stoned them to death. He even held their jackets while they threw the rocks. He hated Christians but he became one. Because', Rob continued, 'he claimed he had met Jesus *after* he was crucified. So did a lot of other people, reliable people, people who were eyewitnesses to the resurrection. More than 500 on one occasion.'

'Paul based his whole argument on the fact that Jesus did rise from the dead.'

'He says, in his First Letter to the Christians in Corinth *(I Corinthians, chapter 15 if you want to look it up)*, that Christians are fools if they preach Jesus was raised from the dead if he actually wasn't.'

'The evidence backs up the claims if you investigate it. Christianity is an evidence-based faith. It stands up to scrutiny if you care to look. And, in fact mate, if the resurrection is *not* true, then I will give up studying to be a minister.'

These conversations went on for months. At times I would say, 'Look, mate, I don't want to hear another word about Christianity! I'm sick of this conversation' and he would say 'Fair enough' and we'd drop the subject for a few weeks; but the questions kept coming back to me and I kept inviting him back to the Pizza Hut.

At first, I was angry at the whole situation I found myself in. Not at Rob or Wendy, but at their faith. This was the main obstacle to me getting back the relationship with Wendy. She continued to refuse to go out with me. I kept going to church because she was there. I didn't know what else to do. She kept being nice to me, she would talk to me, but she wouldn't go out with me. So, somewhat begrudgingly, I did what Forsyth had suggested.

I began investigating the evidence. I read John Stott's *Basic Christianity*. I read C. S. Lewis' *Mere Christianity*. I read *Who Moved the Stone?* written by an investigative lawyer, Frank Morison, who set out to disprove the resurrection himself, using the evidence available, as though he was arguing a case in court and then, in the course of his investigation, came to the realisation that it *must* be true and became a Christian. I read books by Michael Green – *Man Alive, Runaway World, New Life – New Lifestyle*.

And as I read, I started to get a sneaking suspicion that it just might be true. But I didn't want it to be true. I was happy to believe in a God who was out there, somewhere. As long as he left me alone. As long as it didn't affect my life too much.

And then I almost died.

HARD TO CHANGE DIRECTION

It happened late on a Friday afternoon.
I was riding home on my motorbike after the day at the Dental Hospital and I was probably going a bit faster than I should have been. It was drizzling rain and the road was slippery. I was coming through the main street of Ashfield when suddenly a bus, coming from the opposite direction, began to make a right-hand turn into a side street, directly in front of me.

I applied the brakes, and as I did so, the back wheel slid sideways. The bike went down. I hit the bitumen on my right side and began sliding along the slippery wet road towards the back of the turning bus. 'This is it', I thought.

I went under the bus. Just behind the left back wheel. My books and belongings went flying in all directions as the bike came to a halt. The bus driver continued on, unaware an accident had just happened. Lying in the middle of the road, relief rushed through my body.

'I'm still alive!'

Lots of parts of me were hurting. The traffic had stopped, people were gathering to look.

This all happened in front of the Ashfield Pub in the main street with several Aussie blokes outside under the awning having a beer and a smoke. But the first person who came running out to help me was a diminutive

Catholic nun. She eased me to my feet and guided me to the footpath. She collected the books that were scattered across the road.

One of the drinkers came, up-righted my motorbike, and got it off the road. The traffic moved off and the crowd that had gathered started to drift away. The nun asked if I was OK. I assured her that I was. I was sore, but nothing seemed broken, so she wished me well and left me sitting on the edge of the road. After some time to process the accident, I started the bike and headed back to college but very slowly and very carefully.

That night I was lying in bed turning the accident over in my head again and again. I thought, 'If what Forsyth says is true, and I had been killed, I would have been on the down escalator'. That thought kept coming back over the weekend and quite disturbed me!

Monday morning, I arrived at the Dental Hospital and ran into Roger Phillips in the basement at the lockers.

'Rog, I almost got killed on the way home on Friday night.'

I told him the story. Roger and I had become close friends and we'd had many conversations over previous months. He was an agnostic of sorts too *and* he had started seeing a Christian girl called Margaret. He was having a similar problem (*the 'I can't go out with you because you're not a Christian' problem*), I was having with Wendy. 'What is it with these Christian girls?' we asked each other. We shared the books Forsyth had recommended. We commiserated with each other and discussed the whole situation and the ins-and-outs of Christianity numerous times.

He listened to the story of my accident and agreed I'd been very lucky. We briefly discussed the issue of what happens after death. Then shrugged our shoulders, putting those thoughts in the 'too hard' basket, and headed to the sixth floor for a lecture.

That night, 20th September 1970, I gave in.

C S Lewis called himself 'a reluctant convert' when he became a Christian and that about summed up what I felt. After dinner I returned to my room at college, still really disturbed, and feeling a bit stupid, I knelt by my bed and I prayed for the first time in a long time.

HARD TO CHANGE DIRECTION

It was an 'if' – 'if' – 'if' – 'then' prayer.

It went something along the lines of: 'OK God, if you are really there, and if Jesus is really God in person, and if his death was somehow the way for me to be forgiven for the sins that I knew I had committed over my 22 years of life … then please forgive me and change me.'

There was no flash of lightning.

I must admit I didn't feel much different when I got to my feet, but I knew I had to ring Wendy. I went to the payphone down the corridor and rang Wendy's number. When she answered, I blurted out, 'Wendy … I've become a Christian. You can go out with me now.' Her response rather surprised me. 'That's great, but I don't believe you. Prove it.'

We talked for a long time. There was obviously still hope for the relationship, I sensed. But I pondered her challenge. How do I prove it?

After I told Wendy, I headed down to Forsyth's room to tell him the good news! 'Touls, old mate, that's great … but', he added, 'it's not going to be easy. We'll need to keep talking.'

From that moment on, there was a change happening. Fast in some areas of my life. *Somehow*, my swearing stopped almost immediately. Other areas of my life were slower, but nonetheless an overall change *was* taking place. My priorities started to change. I shared my news with Roger and with another dental student, Bob Oliver, who was a keen Christian.

I continued going to church but it suddenly started to mean something other than the opportunity to see Wendy. I began actually studying the Bible with help from others in a group and began helping in the youth group Friday nights.

My study habits improved, and I passed Third Year exams no problem.

CROWNS AND GOWNS
RINGS AND HIGHLAND FLINGS

1972 At the start of my fifth and final year in dentistry, another thing happened that would impact my career as a dentist and as a dental educator in Africa some forty-three years later.
On one of my trips back to Wollongong, I met Anne, one of my Mt Ousley youth-fellowship group, who had married in the meantime. We shared news of the intervening years as our lives had gone in different directions. I told her I was in final year dentistry. Her face lit up.

'Oh, you should contact my brother-in-law, Guenther. He is a dental technician in Park Street Sydney. He's Swiss and very precise. His work, I'm told, is very impressive. He'd be a great mentor.'

I left the Dental Hospital one afternoon and headed uptown. I found the address in Park Street, caught the lift to the fifth floor and poked my head round the door, quickly taking in what was obviously a very sophisticated dental laboratory.

A man wearing loupes, close-up lenses on his glasses, was working at a bench waxing up a five-unit bridge. He was blonde, his hair thinning a little. He looked fit but somewhat tired. Anne had told me he pushed himself far too hard and worked long after his staff. The technicians he employed went home at 5pm. As I entered, he looked up, removed the glasses, and stood up smiling. I tentatively introduced myself. He responded warmly.

'Hi Graham. I'm Guenther. Anne told me about you. I'd be happy to help with your laboratory work if you want to come any day after 5pm when you finish at the Dental Hospital. I'm usually working here till 10pm each night. You could come five nights a week if you wanted. I can always find something for you to do.'

That was the start of a working relationship that went on all year and contributed hugely to my skills in 'Crown and Bridge' and denture work. He was tough. He would give me a gold crown to wax-up and I would do my best and when I thought it was good, I'd proudly give it to him to check. He would look at it and say with a smile, 'Yes, that's pretty good … but I know you can do better.'

And with that he would pick up his wax knife, place it in the flame, and then sink the hot knife into my 'masterpiece' and destroy it. 'Try again' he would say and return to his work. I was shocked, but after some time I could see the difference. My old school motto was 'Age Quod Agis' (whatever you do, do well). That's what Guenther modelled.

(Forty-three years later, I was using that same hot wax knife technique with my students in the middle of Africa. They too were not impressed the first time!)

It was in July of that year (1972) that I proposed to Wendy. It was a very romantic setting on an over-crowded commuter train on the Epping Line. We were coming into Strathfield station. We were packed in like sardines and I whispered the big question in her ear. There was a good deal of blushing and the answer was in the positive, but unlike in today's world, it was not shared with the other commuters. Wendy's parents were surprised and, at the same time, not surprised.

We bought the ring, and as Wendy would be teaching in 1973, picked the first Saturday in the May school holidays for our wedding day. Exciting, but for the moment, final year exams took precedence over wedding plans.

The *Sydney Morning Herald* made us both very happy in December that year, and 1973 saw graduations for both Wendy and me with academic gowns, photos, smiles, handshakes, and congratulations. Most of all, happy parents, and a happy couple.

'Don't settle down in suburbia!' boomed the Reverend Peter Boase enthusiastically from the pulpit on our wedding day. He paused. 'Go out and do something different with your life!' Exhorting us in his sermon with the Bible passage from Micah 6 verse 8 to act justly, love mercy and walk humbly with our God.

Not long after we were married, I was offered the role of 'Junior Dentist' on the Travelling Dental Clinic. A dental clinic in a train carriage that travelled around the state of New South Wales, stopping for days or weeks in a country town, depending on the population, treating pensioners and other needy patients. It would be an adventure. The downside was that Wendy would have to take leave from her job and we'd need to move to the various country towns where the train stopped. 'Why not?', we thought, 'isn't that what Peter Boase was talking about?' We decided we'd give it a go.

Three weeks in the country town of Young, then a month in Yass, where our accommodation was in the caravan park on the edge of the highway, with semi-trailers screeching their brakes all night as they descended the hill alongside.

When the train carriage pulled into Goulburn station on a sunny but chilly winter's day in August, the crowd waiting to register was so large the senior dentist told the team we would be in Goulburn for at least three months. Wendy and I went looking for a flat. No more caravans, Goulburn was even colder than Yass.

We found a little flat opposite the swimming pool. *(We were never tempted to use that facility in the time we were there.)*

From Goulburn, the carriage moved south to Cooma. This was our final destination with the Travelling Dental Clinic. The overall experience for me as a young dentist in a somewhat remote setting was a good one. The grateful country patients often brought gifts of their produce and the occasional large trout. It was a learning experience for both of us and one we never regretted.

In my first year as a dentist, I joined the Christian Dental Fellowship (CDF). It has long since become part of the larger Christian Medical Fellowship but in the 1970s, it was a separate organisation, largely driven by the limitless energy and enthusiasm of Michael Payne. It was through this organisation I realised the opportunities to use my dental skills. 'Volunteering' in your annual holidays caught my imagination and I asked Michael about the possibilities for Wendy and myself, looking ahead to the following January.

He explained there was an opportunity in the highlands of Papua New Guinea at a mission base for the Wycliffe Bible Translators. In this tropical and mountainous country to Australia's north, was a 'town of missionaries', a large contingent of Bible translators, together with support personnel, including pilots, mechanics, teachers, doctors and nurses, printers, along with their children, but at that time, no dentist. Would Wendy and I be interested in doing a month's dentistry there?

It sounded exciting, an adventure where we could do some good, so we 'signed up'. We flew into Port Moresby, and then were flown by light plane, a small Cessna, to Ukarumpa. By road, the journey could take days but with the missionary plane we were there in an hour. Flying can be dangerous in the New Guinea Highlands, we'd heard, with rapid weather changes and low clouds hiding mountain peaks and ridges, so there was a little nervousness as we climbed to altitude and headed away from the coastal fringe. Looking down at picturesque villages below and surrounding jungle, there was also mounting excitement.

That month in Ukarumpa exceeded our expectations. Lots to do at first organising a dental clinic in the Medical Centre. Then, with Wendy acting as 'dental assistant', we got to work treating the large number of men, women, and children, close to 1000. Most of them came for three years or more, from all around the world, so getting regular dental check-ups and routine treatment was difficult in this remote location. The Americans had provided a dental chair and some equipment. I brought along the needed dental materials, donated to the CDF by supporters. The work was interesting and not all dental. I was called upon by the doctor to help put a dislocated shoulder back into place. 'Clunk' – amazing!

Our first Saturday night, we experienced a traditional PNG 'Sing Sing' in a nearby village. Climbing out of the old Land Rover, we were immediately surrounded by a large group of dancers, impressively festooned in bird of paradise plumage, minimal clothing, and many of the men looking rather ferocious with large bones through their nasal septums. This was our first 'culture shock' experience, an event in *stark* contrast to the traditional Australian wedding and reception we had attended in Sydney the previous Saturday night!

After work hours, there was time for fun. With some of the young guys on motorbikes, we explored villages in the hills surrounding Ukarumpa, racing through the tall kunai grasslands and often coming home covered in mud. The hospitality shown to us, sharing meals in many homes, was overwhelming. We returned to Australia keen to do it all again the following January.

These experiences – the adventure of 'mission'; flying by light plane to remote mountainous regions; setting up dental clinics, more or less, from scratch; having to improvise when you don't have everything you *think* you need; the spontaneity and random-ness of life; the motorbikes, the mud and the kunai grass; the camaraderie of the people with whom you work; but most importantly, the feeling that you are doing something that matters – all these things had an impact on us. After the second visit, we explored the possibility of returning for two years as the 'resident dentist', but an American dentist was already 'in the pipeline'. One door closed.

But another door was about to open.

LONDON DETOUR

OVERLAND FROM KATHMANDU

1976 After almost three years of marriage we did what many other Aussies did back then. We booked a trip to London. But not just a 24-hour flight. Our trip would end up taking 106 days and would mean travelling through 21 countries. A trip no longer possible.

We left family and friends and flew out of Sydney on Monday, the 9th of February, intending to be away from Australia for about a year. We had pushed the short-term mission door and it didn't open. We'd talked about the guidance of God with older, more mature Christian friends and, as we still didn't know what God wanted us to do, we decided to follow what *we* wanted to do. The plan we came up with was to travel overland to London, work for a year, and then think about returning home. (We were to discover the truth of Proverbs 16 verse 9 – people make their plans, but God directs their steps.)

Arriving in Singapore we meandered our way round the fascinating city, seeing the sights, sweating in the humidity, enjoying the food from the street markets, and just soaking up the culture. We then headed north up the peninsula, with a taxi driver who seemed to have a death wish – overtaking at speed on blind corners, pulling out to pass with overloaded logging trucks bearing down on us. To our surprise and relief, we arrived safely in Kuala Lumpur, but decided to *fly* to Nepal.

Flying into the Himalayas, the seat belt sign came on indicating turbulence. As the pilot guided the Thai Airlines plane over a massive mountain ridge, the aircraft hit an air pocket and suddenly dropped several hundred metres. People screamed and frantically looked at each other; Wendy and I held hands. The pilot regained control and we came into land. Spontaneous applause broke out as the intercom announced: 'Welcome to Kathmandu'.

Kathmandu, in 1976, was drawing 'hippies', tourists, trekkers, mountain-climbers and 'overlanders' like us from all over the world. The airport was buzzing as we collected our luggage and prepared to enter what we had heard was an ancient world, expecting to step back in time. Changing some American dollars into rupees, we left the airport, looking with first-time wonder at the incredible mountain ranges surrounding and dwarfing this medieval capital of Nepal. Trying not to look too much like naïve tourists, despite the backpacks and the camera, we began the airport routine, looking for a reputable taxi man. We made it to the hotel without parting with too many extra rupees and researched a good place to eat in *The Student Guide to Asia*, which had many suggestions, not all of them recommended. We chose the 'new style pie shop', known as the *Chi and Pie* which the guidebook described as 'located in a grotty little side street'.

The guidebook also had some 'health hints': 'Do not drink unboiled water in Nepal; stick to tea, coffee, hot lemon etc. Water in restaurants is rarely boiled. *(This was in the days before 'bottled water'.)* Hepatitis and gastroenteritis are rife in the more squalid areas of Kathmandu (especially around the *Oriental Hotel* where the 'hippies' hang out) and travellers should be careful, especially when eating and smoking communal joints.'

We found out about the gastroenteritis often in the coming days, and we avoided the joints, as we wandered the streets of Kathmandu, enjoying the sights, taking lots of photographs, and meeting other members of the group that would take the *Capricorn* bus to London. Bill, the driver, was a typical Aussie adventurer of the time, with long hair, beard, ragged jeans, and a laconic attitude to life – except when driving, when he became very focussed. Alistair, the courier, was a Londoner. He had to worry about getting everyone on the bus, keeping everyone happy, searching out who was dragging the chain and, ahead, getting everyone across the many borders to come.

Wednesday, 25th February, our pre-departure meeting. We contributed 400 American dollars into the 'kitty' for our camping-style accommodation on the second part of the trip, from Iran onwards. *(Having that money in kitty turned out to be very good forward planning.)*

The day before departure, Bill had organised a tour of nearby temples and the Tibetan refugee compound. At the Hindu temple, Pashupatinath, we saw a sight that we couldn't get out of our minds.

Bill parked the bus on the hillside a short distance from the temple. We descended and were approaching the temple, taking photographs. To the right of the path there was a prayer mat with a raised area of dirt about the size of a grave. Sticking out of the 'grave' was what looked like a chunky branch intertwined with a string of beads. As we came closer, we realised it wasn't a branch, it was a human hand.

'What? It can't be' we thought, trying to make sense of what our eyes were seeing. And then the fingers of the hand started moving, fingering the beads.

'What *is* this?'

I approached a nearby Hindu man and asked, 'What's going on here?' He replied along the lines of, 'He's doing "puja" for his sins.'

'Really?' I replied, still mystified, 'but, how long will he be down there?' 'Two or three months' was the unconcerned reply. 'Two or three *months*? But won't he die?' I asked plaintively. He shrugged his shoulders. 'Maybe'. We couldn't see any way he could breathe or eat …

One of the group shattered our sense of dismay with, 'Let's go stomp on his fingers.' … There's one in every group.

A new culture and a religion we didn't understand. *(In the days to come, we were to see up-close a variety of the world's religions, suffer from recurrent sickness and run out of money.)*

SPLENDOUR AND SICKNESS

The day of departure dawned fine but hazy, the towering Himalayan mountains barely visible. After an early breakfast, we packed the bus, passing our duffel bags and suitcases up to some of the intrepid girls standing on the roof. Then the 28 passengers climbed aboard the *Capricorn Tour Bus* and found their seats. A few last-minute instructions over the PA system and Bill started the engine. Our overland trip had begun!

We made our way through the narrow cobble-stoned streets, and soon, had left the ancient city far behind. Driving on the precarious roads climbing out of the Kathmandu Valley, looking over the edge of the cliffs dropping away hundreds of metres from the side of the bus where we were sitting, was a nerve-wracking experience. At times the bus swayed precariously on the narrow road to avoid oncoming traffic, causing our adrenaline levels to rise and our eyes to widen, but we eventually made it to Pokhara by mid-afternoon.

The trip from Pokhara to the Indian border and on to Gorakhpur took most of the following day. 'The rustic hotel', I wrote in my diary, 'was surprisingly clean'.

Then it was on to Benares, stopping for lunch at Sarnath, where it was reported Buddha had preached his first sermon 2500 years before. Benares, otherwise known as Varanasi, the Holy City of the Hindus, was rated along with Damascus as one of the world's oldest cities. Every

Hindu, we were told, wishes to die in Benares and have his or her body burnt on the *ghats* that border the river Ganges, their ashes being scattered on the holy river where, it is said, *karma* is achieved.

It was here in Benares the problems that create the adventures of travel started to present themselves.

The first was finding a hotel. Apparently, the *Mint House* had been rebooked for a wedding party. 'I am sorry sir, but there is no room for your group.'

'Where do we spend the night?' After making some enquiries, Bill and Alistair were directed to the *King's Guest House*, a once-stately mansion which had fallen into a state of disrepair over the fourteen years since Queen Elizabeth had stayed there in 1962. It was fitted out with beautiful cedar furniture and long banquet tables, reminiscent of its bygone splendour.

Following dinner, the second problem arose. It concerned our accommodation and, more specifically, the toilets. As there were few bedrooms, we slept in dormitories. It helped us getting to know our fellow travellers, for better or worse. But *our* dorm was next to one of only two toilets and meant a steady stream of visitors rushing through and a terrible night's sleep. So we were not sad when Bill came at 5.30am to tell us all to 'get out of bed, we're going to the ghats'.

The ghats are the terraced steps that lead down to the Ganges where Hindus pray at dawn, do their ablutions, and where the dead are continually being cremated.

As we leave Benares, the road out of town is blocked by elephants. The bus stops and various people are vomiting. One of them, Rick, an American about 28 years old, is seriously ill and has no medication. His face sunken with dark rings under his eyes.

A few days of travel from Benares we reached one of the major highlights of this long stretch: the Taj Mahal. Magnificent, even with bamboo scaffolding in the main porch. We spent a very pleasant evening hour strolling the gardens, admiring the architecture, and examining the beautiful white marble tomb of Shah Jahan's favourite wife who had died while giving birth to her fourteenth child.

SPLENDOUR AND SICKNESS

We had a wide range of people on our bus, from Australia and overseas. One couple, who had done a lot of travelling, (but had never seen the Taj before or even been to India), seemed impatient to get back to the hotel. When we asked them if they had explored the inside of the Taj, they replied they didn't need to as they had seen it all in art books!

Dinner at the *Kwality Restaurant*, reportedly one of the best English type restaurants in Agra, seemed good, but you never knew until the next day!

During a tour of the palace at Fatehpuhr Sikri, 27 km from Agra, I started to feel a little 'off'. But soon the bus was off again, to the Prime Minister's Mausoleum and the Red Fort. During the tour of the Mausoleum, waves of nausea and sweating overcame me. I adjourned to the lawn, where I found others in the same condition, and by the time we got to the Red Fort, I could barely stand but did manage to see the room where Shah Jahan died, with a view of his beloved marble masterpiece in the distance.

(He had plans to build a black mirror-image Taj on the other side of the river for his own tomb with a silver bridge connecting the two. However, the people revolted at the huge expense and the suffering caused by building the white Taj, and he was imprisoned in the Red Fort.)

I thought a cold Coke might settle my stomach, but it only made things worse, and in the car park, with a beautiful view of the Taj, I was violently ill.

The next day we were all back on board the bus, well or otherwise, heading for Jaipur known as 'the pink city', and then on to the Indian capital, New Delhi, arriving late in the afternoon. We were tired, but there was still a degree of excitement, as this would be our first mail stop. Yes, letters! *(1976, long before mobile phones or internet.)* Such an encouragement to read the ten letters that were waiting from home.

My diary for that day carries an interesting note: 'One of the girls saw me reading the John Blanchard book, *Right with God* and asked if it was fiction or non-fiction.'

As we were leaving the restaurant that night, we had a chance conversation with an American lady. She was a missionary and invited us to the Delhi Bible Fellowship meeting, 6pm Sunday evening at the *Imperial Hotel*.

The following day, Sunday, Bill had organised a morning tour which included Raj-Ghat, where Gandhi was cremated after his assassination on the 30th January 1948. Then in the evening we found our way to the *Imperial Hotel*. The sermon was on Nehemiah's rebuilding the walls around Jerusalem after they had been destroyed by the Babylonians. The main point was perseverance in the task that God had given Nehemiah despite ridicule, force, dissension, discouragement, compromise with the world and false prophets, until the task was completed. The message and conversation with a lovely Indian Christian man after the meeting really encouraged us.

We had a good meal that night and slept well.

THE KHYBER PASS AND BEYOND

In the weeks that followed we travelled through the north of India, to Amritsar, visiting the Golden Temple of the Sikhs, and on to Jammu. From there we headed further up into the Himalayas to Srinagar, the capital of Kashmir where we spent several very chilly days on houseboats on the Dal Lake, visiting the snowfields at Gulmarg, the last part of the journey on horseback.

From India we crossed into Pakistan visiting Lahore and on to Peshawar via Rawalpindi. Meals, over these weeks, were a bit like a game of Russian roulette. It appears from my diary, that on any given day either Wendy was sick, or I was sick, or we were both sick!

Crossing the Indus River, Mike, one of our group, who was a bit of an expert on British war history, with a tendency towards theatrical dramatization, felt he could 'almost hear the invading armies marching through the gorge'. The massive Indus River is deep blue and where it meets the dirty brown, turbulent water of the Kabul River, an impressive sight.

From Peshawar, we headed into interesting and impressive landscapes. As we travel up the Khyber Pass, where so many historic battles have taken place, Mike takes over the microphone in the bus and describes in amazing detail some of the battles that have occurred. There are sheer shale cliffs rising on both sides above the serpentine road, winding its way between never-ending mountains. On the vast brown plains in between the peaks, box-like mud houses are scattered. We head ever upwards, past the Khyber Rifles Fort, donkey caravans winding their way along rocky tracks in the heights above us, fat-tailed sheep along the side of the road, and we arrive at the Afghan border, where we wait two and a half hours to cross. The bus looks like a hospital ward, with suffering people scattered throughout, some grumbling, some groaning, many sleeping. We buy some afghani bread and meat, a Central Asia 'hamburger', and drink the best chai we've ever tasted.

Crossing a vast stony desert, we pass through the magnificent grandeur of the Kabul Gorge before arriving in Kabul. It's very similar to Kashmir, surrounded with bare trees, snow-capped hills, and filled with bleak houses.

But we awake the next day to magnificent clear blue skies, white snow, and a ring of mountains. Kabul is another mail stop, and we are excited at the prospect but disappointed with the result. Feeling quite low, we walk into a steak house. Then a bearded guy, heavily rugged-up against the cold, speaks to me as I pass:

'How ya goin' Touls?'

It was a friend from dentistry, Jim Horan. With Jim were Anna and Arno, also friends from university days. They joined us for dinner. To complete the, 'it's a small world' experience, in downtown Kabul, Wendy meets a friend from her Cheltenham Girls High School days now on her way back to Australia from England. Unbelievable!

From Kabul, we climbed slowly to 7500 ft (2300 m), travelling through vast wastelands of snow on a plateau ringed by mountains, stopping at a *caravanserai* for lunch. When we arrive in Kandahar, we are both sick.

The following day we face a 586 km stretch across the *Desert of Death*. We leave early with only a cup of chai for breakfast. But we're stopped by flooding ... *flooding* in the Desert of Death!

It turns into a comfort stop. But in the middle of a desert with no toilets and not a single tree in sight ... So, 'girls to the right of the bus, boys to the left' caused welcome relief and not a little awkwardness.

To get through the floods it was necessary to unload all the suitcases from under the bus and strap them on top. We weren't too happy that night finding our sleeping bags were wet – they had been left *under* the bus.

We came across several casualties caused by the flash flooding. An Iranian double container truck had jack-knifed and was bogged on both sides of the bitumen highway. Two front-end loaders were finally able to clear the road and enable us to get through but for some time it was a comedy of errors. Another Iranian carrier had been washed *off* the road and was resting on its side. The desert was bleak, but the sunset was magnificent. We crawled into Herat at 9pm after a tortuous 13½ hours on the road, only to find the hotel room smelt, with an abominable toilet that was completely blocked, unable to be flushed!

By arriving at the Iranian border early, it only took us five hours to cross! At the border-post was a 'drug museum' with exhibits of the many ways travellers, overlanders and hippies had tried to smuggle drugs into Iran and been caught. A Kombi van ripped apart revealing secret compartments loaded with drugs. There were shoes with false heels, hollowed-out wooden crutches. The penalties were harsh, and Bill warned the group not to try carrying marijuana across the border. We crossed safely and then found to the group's outrage, someone had indeed brought drugs across. We could *all* have been imprisoned.

It was snowing as we arrived in Mashhad, and by morning there was six inches of snow on the ground. It was extremely cold, the floor of the bus was wet, and everyone is freezing and miserable. We are headed for Tehran via the Caspian Sea. Crossing the mountain pass at 9000 ft (2743 m) we arrive in the outskirts of Tehran late afternoon.

We had organised for family in Australia to send money to the American Express Office in Tehran *(that's the way it was done back in the 1970's)* so, the following day we eagerly arrived at the American Express Office only to find our money had not arrived. This bombshell rocked us. We withdrew to a coffeehouse, ordered, and then contemplated the rest of the trip. 'What do we do now?' Other members of our group found us, and suggested we join them to see the Iranian Crown Jewels. We agree, although we were still in shock and feeling very depressed.

The Iranian Crown Jewels were kept deep underground in a bank vault. Jewel-encrusted cups, sabres, saddle pommels, dishes, armour, crowns, a solid gold peacock throne encrusted with every sort of precious stone you could imagine and a solid gold globe of the world a metre in diameter, with the countries defined by rubies and the oceans and seas emeralds. The largest ruby in the world was there along with the largest pink diamond, and everywhere gold bowls filled with precious gems – diamonds, rubies, amethysts, emeralds. We left staggered at the wealth that was beneath that bank.

In complete contrast, our hotel was dingy, situated over a rundown garage, but it did have one redeeming feature. At breakfast the next morning, there was a box of *Kellogg's Corn Flakes*. 'Seconds?' … 'Don't mind if I do.'

On the road again, heading 400 km south to Isfahan. As we arrived, two of the girls realised they had left their passports in Tehran! The only solution was to catch the night bus back to Tehran. Fortunately, the group was staying in Isfahan for three nights, so they were able to retrieve them and return before the bus left for the next destination.

At this stage, money, or the lack thereof, was often on our minds. We had contacted Wendy's parents to recover the money sent to Tehran and resend it to Damascus as there was a double opportunity to pick it up. Our tour was due to arrive in Damascus on April 20th, fly to Egypt for ten days, then back to Damascus, so we reasoned, if we missed the money the first time through, we would certainly pick it up on our return.

Isfahan was a beautiful city, magnificent mosques, exquisite mosaic work, friendly and welcoming people. We enjoyed the city, and we enjoyed the *Shah Jahan Hotel*, reputed to be one of the most beautiful in the world. Of course, we couldn't afford to stay there or even eat a meal there, but we did find that coffee was affordable; and it was our 'go-to' place in those three days especially when we needed clean toilets. We would sink into the plush lounges and enjoy the ambience, sipping our expensive coffees, writing letters home, avoiding the staff who kept enquiring if we needed anything, and then supplementing our meagre supply of toilet paper as we left. Quite a contrast with the Youth Hostel where we were staying!

In Isfahan, we celebrated my 28th birthday, but there was no breakfast in bed; in fact, there was no breakfast. However, letters from home and the pianist at the Shah Jahan Hotel playing *Happy Birthday* to me on the grand piano, made for some nice birthday surprises.

THE KHYBER PASS AND BEYOND

Persepolis was our first attempt at camping, and with the hard ground, tent pegs that bent, and our lack of experience, there was quite a bit of hilarity. The ruins of Persepolis date back to 515 BC. The last Shah of Iran celebrated the 2500th Anniversary of the Persian Empire in 1971, five years before our visit. He was forced into exile in 1979, the beginning of the Islamic Republic of Iran.

It was at these magnificent ruins of Persepolis that we reached new depths with our lack of money and our need to survive. Three ladies from an English tour group, put their unfinished drinks on a nearby table and moved off. We moved in, fast, and finished them off. They were delicious.

Iran passes into Iraq, the days long, the scenery uninspiring, sandy plains and date palms, the group of travellers getting more irritated with each other. We are keen to get to Jerusalem, but it is still over a week away.

Baghdad is 'underwhelming'. We're in the 'camping stage' now and on reaching the camping ground find it flooded, so we pitch between the puddles. A daytrip to Babylon, 85 km from Baghdad, but it too is a disappointment, just piles of rubble, no longer one of the *Seven Wonders of the World*. On returning to our camp, we find the tents ransacked and Bob has lost two pairs of underpants! We left Baghdad dispirited and homesick.

It's a glorious relief to leave Iraq, and the scenery changes again as we cross into Jordan. The border a black rock desert, basalt, as far as the eye can see. Amman, the capital of Jordan, is the halfway point of our trip, and the next mail stop. Five letters, and our mood lifts. Here Wendy is asked if she would like to be the third wife of a 'gentleman' who stopped us in the street … she declines graciously.

On to Aqaba on the gulf where the beach is littered with rubbish, but the crystal-clear waters are delightful to swim in and we start to feel refreshed and rejuvenated. People on the bus begin to argue over whether to stay at the beach another day and eliminate Petra from the itinerary, but the majority vote for Petra.

Petra is spectacular, the most famous site in Jordan. You enter the hidden city via a narrow canyon between the pink sandstone and granite cliffs that tower 300 ft (90 m) above you. Through this canyon come glimpses of a massive structure carved out of the cliffs. *The Treasury*, known as *Al-Khazneh*, stands 150 ft (45 m) high and was carved out of the rock in 300 BC.

Backtracking to Amman, where one of our group was forced to fly to London with hepatitis. This return to Amman, meant another opportunity for letters at the *Poste Restante,* sadly, none about the money transfer. But our disappointment is overshadowed by the prospect of crossing to the *West Bank* the next morning and heading up to Jerusalem. We are excited as the itinerary has been slightly changed so we spend the whole of Easter in Jerusalem.

EASTER IN JERUSALEM

Four hours to cross the Jordanian Israeli border and waiting on the other side were a fleet of Mercedes taxis. Climbing aboard this luxury transport, we sink into the plush leather seats and a huge weight of stress seemed to lift.

Driving through the hills of Israel, past Jericho, finally catching a glimpse of Jerusalem was a wonderful experience, especially for Wendy and me, two young keen Christians. This is the place where it all happened. Our spirits were high, elated at being here for Easter. It was not time-tabled that way when we saw the original itinerary in Australia, but the route was rearranged and we now were arriving on Wednesday the 14th April 1976, two days before Good Friday.

We had hoped to be on our own as it would have been easier to find accommodation for two, but we couldn't leave our friends in the taxi. So, our group of five, Mike, Deb, Robyn and the two of us, were on the lookout for somewhere to stay, anywhere. The city was packed with pilgrims, people going in all directions, pushing and shoving, shouting and gesticulating. We asked many people where we might find some accommodation but with no success. After some time, 'providence' took over. We realised Robyn was missing. Two Jewish boys stopped us and asked if we had lost a friend. They led us through the crowd right to her. She hugged us all, greatly relieved. The boys become our 'de facto accommodation guides', expecting a little something if they help us. They took us to the Lutheran Hostel. It was full. They knew one more place nearby and urged us to follow them. It's getting close to dark. They took us to a house in the middle of the *Old City*. We knocked on the door and a man about 60 years old in a fur hat came to the door, smiled, greeted us, and then, with his hands palm up says, 'Sorry but there's no room here.'

Maybe it was our downcast looks and obvious growing despair that caused him to look inside, then back at us and then, with a wide grin: 'If you don't mind being 'squashed', we can find a way to help. By the way, my name is complicated, you can call me Mister A.' Taking us *all* to his bedroom, he explained the sleeping arrangements: 'You can sleep two to each single bed, one of you can sleep on the floor and I will sleep on the windowsill', and that is what we did. Clean toilets and hot showers, a delicious meal, and our three travelling companions were amazed with these 'coincidences' which *we* called 'providence'.

What a significant Easter this is going to be. We didn't know how special.

I rose at 6am and wandered through the deserted ancient city, taking the *Via Dolorosa* down to *Lions Gate*. I sat on a small stone wall, lost in thought. Easter. In Jerusalem. An hour of reflection later I headed back for breakfast.

Climbing into another of those Mercedes taxis, we headed out of the city. First stop, Bethlehem, the place where Jesus was born. Then on to Hebron to the tombs of Abraham, Isaac, Jacob and Joseph, heroes of the Old Testament; stopping at *Solomon's Pools* where an aqueduct once supplied water for the entire city of Jerusalem. The countryside is beautiful, changing from green slopes to more desert country as we travelled south to the *Dead Sea*. A short detour to Sodom on the way where our taxi driver points out a pillar of salt, calling it 'Lot's wife'!

Time for a dip in the Dead Sea, a fun flotation experience with both our arms and legs sticking out of the water and not sinking. The water feels oily and stings your eyes with its high salt content. We head back to Jerusalem via Jericho, in time for the Communion Service at *Christ Church* in the old city, just around the corner from our accommodation, followed by a walk to Gethsemane.

EASTER IN JERUSALEM

Good Friday we woke early, joining a devotional walk along the *Via Dolorosa* – a poignant time reflecting on the lead up to the crucifixion. From there, we headed to the 9am Good Friday Service in *Christ Church*. The minister announced the first hymn and we stood to sing. Two people asked to squeeze past us into the pew and we turned to face them, … we don't believe it. It was my dental mate, Bob Oliver, and his wife Chris. We embraced, tears rolling down our cheeks, making so much noise the congregation turned round to see what the commotion was all about. *(Bob and Chris have been living in north London and were due to return to Australia when we arrived and took over their flat. We knew they were travelling at this time but had no idea of their itinerary.)*

We spent the day wandering the cobble-stoned streets of the *Old City* together, walking the city wall, drinking gallons of coffee, talking, catching up, and later in the day sharing a fish dinner.

Easter Sunday, we woke very early, and, trying not to wake the others, headed off for the Easter Sunday Service at the *Garden Tomb*. A joyful and deeply moving experience. We again spent the day with Bob and Chris, exploring Jerusalem, saying our last farewells late in the day after the most memorable Easter we had ever had. How strange, we reflected, that we, travelling from Australia, and they from London, met in Jerusalem, at Easter, without either of us knowing the other would be there.

Tomorrow we meet up with the group again and head back to Amman.

SURVIVAL STRATEGY

At this point of the trip, we still have just over a month to London, in fact, 34 days to survive. Our money is running out. Asking people for money, people who, a few months earlier were complete strangers and who in a month's time, would all go their separate ways in London, didn't appeal to us. We still had the money, we thought, in 'kitty' to cover one good meal a day when camping. The flights, accommodation and tours in Egypt were part of the original ticket price, so we *just* had to find money for food and extras.

With these questions about our survival and an increasing amount of underlying anxiety, we re-joined the group and boarded the bus at the Jordanian border, very happy to push on the next day towards Damascus in Syria, in the hope of retrieving our money at American Express.

Arriving in Damascus our priority is finding the American Express office. We find it, but the money is not there. The agent tells us, in stilted English, to try the Commercial Bank of Syria the next day. On the way back to the camping ground we walk past the 'street called Straight', mentioned in the Acts of the Apostles, where Ananias is told he can find a man named Paul. *(Biblical reminders aplenty in this part of the journey.)*

Our evening meal that night is bread and coffee. The lack of money starting to affect us.

The next morning, at the Commercial Bank of Syria Main Branch, we're told the same story, 'There is no money' ... What do we do?

Our spirits lift when we find eight letters at the *Poste Restante*, with one mentioning 'the money' was resent on the 13th of April. It is now the 21st, so we calculate it should arrive by the time we return from our ten-day tour of Egypt which begins with the flight to Cairo tonight.

On the plane they serve a delicious chicken dinner, and we are full for the first time in days. 'Sweet talking' the air hostess we score five extra packets of biscuits and cheese. A glorious night's sleep in Cairo. Clean sheets, good bed. Then to top it off, a huge continental breakfast.

Bill summons us and we are on our way to Alexandria. We push through the city traffic and leave Cairo behind, the countryside we are entering, lush and green. Crops on the sides of the road, buffalo grazing or pulling ancient ploughs. The Nile alongside, magnificent in the hot Egyptian sun.

In Alexandria, the first stop is King Farouk's Summer House. Not a bad pad for the playboy king to get away from the *stress* of running the country before he was forced to abdicate in 1952. Then a late lunch stop looking out over the Mediterranean. Everyone eats except us. We take a walk, just the two of us, along the seaside and sit on a wall gazing wistfully at the sea. Janet, one of our group, finds us. She realised we weren't with the group, and thoughtfully lends us £5. Dinnertime, we head off downtown alone and buy some falafels, pastries, and banana milk shakes, thanks to Janet's 'fiver'.

The following day we're taken to the Catacombs of Alexandria, Pompey's Pillar, and the Roman amphitheatre and then the bus returns us to Cairo in the afternoon, dropping us at the railway station to catch the night train south to Luxor and the *Valley of the Kings*. The local tour guide is very disorganised, and the general opinion is that he can't be trusted. However, the train departs with all aboard for what seems like the perfect setting for an 'Agatha Christie murder mystery'. The guide is watching his back.

A terrible night's sleep on the train but nobody was murdered. There's no breakfast, so after we arrive in Luxor, we eat some stale bread with a little jam we had brought with us from that large continental breakfast, washed down with a roadside cup of tea.

SURVIVAL STRATEGY

The guide suggests we go to the Son et Lumière (Sound and Light Show) at the Luxor Temple that night, and of course inflates the price of tickets. All the group excepting us, buys into the outing. The group arrives at the Karnak Temple and the 'bus detectives' do their private investigation about ticket costs. They discover the guide's price-gouging, are hopping mad, and decide to confront him. To 'save face' he backs down and refunds all the money he's taken from the group.

Meanwhile we are sitting by the Nile, in the sweltering heat. We don't have the entry fee for the magnificent temple, or later, for the sound and light show. Oh well!

The next day is ANZAC Day, a special day for Australians and New Zealanders, commemorating the battle at Gallipoli and other battle fronts. We will visit Gallipoli in the weeks to come. ANZAC Day is spent crossing the Nile to the *Valley of the Kings* and amongst many other dynastic kings, the impressive tomb of King Tutankhamen. Then it was on to the *Valley of the Queens*, and in particular, Queen Hatshepsut and the tombs of Rameses I, II and III. All so impressive, but tombs can be very tiring if you haven't had enough to eat.

The spectacular sunset over the Nile, with a band playing in the background, was a great moment, then we were headed for the railway station and the return sleep-less trip to Cairo.

It was here we realised the implication of the timing of our return flight to Damascus. It was booked for the coming Friday, but *Friday* is the Muslim holy day, all the banks will be closed, and the bus leaves Damascus midday Friday. We won't be able to access the banks *at all* if we fly Friday.

OK. We approached Alastair and the tour operators to see if we could get an early flight Thursday morning, arriving in Damascus midmorning, giving us the rest of the day to find our money. Alastair said he would get back to us.

Climbing aboard a *felucca* (an ancient sailboat) that afternoon, we crossed the Nile. It was the Egyptian Easter, and the boat was loaded with celebrating Egyptian families.

In the days that followed, our group visited more of the amazing sites of Egypt. The Cairo Museum with the Mummy Room and King

Tutankhamen's treasures, very impressive. Memphis, the ancient capital, 20 km south of Cairo, on the West Bank of the Nile, where the enormous, restored statue of Rameses II was found in the Nile, as well as the Step Pyramid nearby – 5000 years old and the world's first stone building. Then finally, to Giza, the site of the Pyramids and Sphinx. We entered the Great Pyramid and made our way to the burial chamber hidden deep within. What an imposing and impressive building, the stone blocks enormous. The Sphinx was smaller than we had imagined, and at that time, the face and chest were covered in scaffolding. *(We have come to the conclusion on this trip, that half the world's tourist sites are in ruins, and the other half in scaffolding.)*

Climbing Cheops, the Great Pyramid, was too expensive, but throwing caution *and* the budget to the wind, just before sunset I decide to climb Menkaure, the smallest of the three pyramids, 213 ft (65 m) tall. I managed this with a guide who got me to the top even with my fear of heights.

The tour driver is taking the group back to Cairo and Wendy is keen to find out if our flights have been changed, but Rick, Jude and I want to do some more photography, so they left us behind. We lingered until after dark to see if we could photograph the Pyramids and the Sphinx without paying for the Sound and Light show seats. We were successful from a spot near the main stand until a guard discovered us and showed us the door. Finding a taxi, we share the one-Egyptian-pound-ride back to the hotel, very happy with our 'pyramid experience'.

We are booked on the 6.15am flight so will have to be up early. Hallelujah! Let's hope we find the money!

We didn't need an alarm. The nearby mosque started prayers at 3.45am and then the roosters began at 4.30am. We caught a taxi to the airport before dawn and boarded our flight, arriving in Damascus at 8.45.

The big questions were … Where is our money and can we find it? Does anyone speak English? Will anyone help us? We are now on our own, no Alastair or Bill to help with the situation. No-one who knows Damascus or where American Express offices might be located. All we had was a letter saying the money had been sent to American Express.

Through customs, and a bus to the centre of the city where I left Wendy in the foyer of a large hotel with all our baggage, most of which was anxiety. I leapt down the steps of the hotel and began running, frantically asking people 'Where is the American Express office?' Most people I asked spoke no English and just shrugged … Great! Finally, someone knew, and I arrived panting at the counter, but the person behind that counter was neither helpful nor interested.

'No, your money is not here', and I was seemingly dismissed as he turned his head and lifted his coffee cup taking a sip of the treacly black liquid.

'This is not happening' I thought. 'Where might it be?' I asked. He put the cup on his desk and frowned. 'You try Commercial Bank. Maybe it's there, but hurry, they close at midday.' 'Where can I find the Commercial Bank?' I pleaded. 'Down the road, you try there', he said, pointing left. He shrugged and turned back to his coffee.

Panic.

Again, bursting through the front door I turned left and started running as fast as I could. I found the branch down the road. No money. 'Try other Commercial Banks around here' the teller said in broken English, and I pushed out of the bank doors once again, breathing hard, heart rate pounding.

During the next hour until the banks closed, I found five other branches. The Head Office and branches one, two, three, four and six.

No money. Despair. 'How do I tell Wendy?'

(We found out later the money was in Branch five but in the days before internet banking, ATMs, and all the other technological advances of the last 45 years; finding places and information was almost impossible in another language in a strange city.)

I returned to the hotel and broke the bad news to Wendy and for some time we were engulfed in grief.

'What do we do? We've only got 71 American dollars left from our original money and we've still got 25 days of the trip to survive.'

So here we were, in a situation that had never arisen for us before. Full of grief, a situation where the only option we could see was to trust God. In affluent Australia, with family and well-paid jobs, we had never really had to rely on God to provide. Can we make it across Turkey and Europe on a budget of 71 American dollars?

OK! This is what we decided we had to do.

The rules for the remaining money. Spend *no more* than three American dollars a day. No sweets, chocolates or treats. No entry fees into tourist places except for Ephesus – we *can't* miss out on seeing Ephesus. Trust God and keep smiling.

We were to see some interesting things in the days ahead.

TURKISH DELIGHT

Our group arrived from Egypt late on the Friday morning. We climbed aboard the bus, everyone greeted us, and it was assumed we had gotten the money. Bill and Alastair asked us straight out and we told them the bad news along with a few others.

Our destination is northern Syria, the town of Aleppo, before we enter Turkey the following day. After travelling for four hours, we arrive at the Aleppo camping ground where we have the first test of our 'survival budget'. Camping costs four Syrian pounds *each* and our daily limit of three American dollars translates into eleven Syrian pounds so we have about three Syrian pounds (less than a dollar) for food. A nearby shop sells us falafels for under a pound, so we are within budget. It happened to be Labour day and, as we walked along, people gave us nuts and coffee as part of the festivities. We were happy to accept their hospitality. So far, so good.

The border crossing into Turkey was straight-forward, they didn't even bother checking our suitcases or duffel bags. Most of the time was spent changing money *again*. This time into Turkish Lira, sixteen to the dollar.

The countryside we travel through is picturesque – fields with a profusion of red poppies and masses of purple and yellow flowers, the ruins of a Crusader castle on a rocky prominence, terraced hills and then finally we glimpse the Mediterranean Sea.

In the afternoon we arrive at the town of Tarsus, well-known to readers of the Bible as the birthplace of the Apostle Paul. Bill booked us all into a hotel, and as we walked through the lounge, there was a large group of men around a TV set fixated on the FA Cup Final of 1976. Serendipity. How good is this! I join the men and watch Southampton beat Manchester United 1-0.

Dinner is not cooked by the group tonight, so we settle for bread and tomatoes, a hot chocolate, and an orange each. Wendy and Jude asked the restaurant next door if they could warm the milk and they returned with the milk, some Turkish recipes, and an offer from the manager for a night on the town. Thank you. Thank you. Pass.

Back on the bus before 8am our destination today is Ürgüp but we make a stop at the underground city of Kamakli where Christians hid in troglodyte (cave) dwellings from persecution over the centuries. A fascinating place, we were told. We couldn't afford to go in *and* stay 'on-budget'.

The Mo-camp at Ürgüp was excellent with soft ground and hot showers. In the evening we wandered into town and met a local barber called Kardir, who invited us to his grandmother's house for coffee and snacks. It was so enjoyable 'hanging out' with locals who didn't seem to have an agenda, just hospitable people.

I had written in my diary just that morning: 'The doubts are beginning to creep in – it's hard to have faith that God will provide when you are hungry' … Ironic.

The next morning Bill was blowing the horn at 9am and we vied for our favourite seats. First come, best seated, elbow-use optional.

The nearby Goreme Valley is renowned for its natural rock erosions forming what are called 'fairy chimneys'. Wind and water erode the softer sandstone bases of these unusual formations, leaving the much harder basalt caps on top. From the Fourth Century, Christians had carved homes, churches, and isolated cells out of the sandstone walls and religious hermits who considered themselves 'dead to the world' lived here, the earliest forms of what is called 'monasticism'. A fascinating place. An other-worldly valley which caused the astronaut Neil Armstrong, on visiting Goreme, to say 'now I have been to the moon *twice*'. A must-see place for Christians interested in church history. Except for the entrance fee which again didn't fit within our 'survival budget'.

The bus parked in the carpark and our crowd poured out. Wendy and I looked at each other. We knew we couldn't go down and see the Byzantine frescoes in the rock churches *and* eat that day. We chose to eat. But it was a decision that made us miserable, watching all our fellow-travellers paying and then descending into the depths of this unique stone valley.

I stared at my boots and wandered over to the mesh fence to see if I could push my camera through and sneak a few shots.

Meanwhile, buses were pulling up and disgorging masses of tourists down the steep little staircase. Wendy had wandered off exploring the car park and after 20 minutes or so I went looking for her and spied her over by the side of one of the buses talking to a man in his mid-40s.

She saw me and beckoned me over.

'Gra, this is Bill Conover' she said.

"Hi Bill' I replied, shaking his hand.

'Very pleased to meet you and your lovely wife Wendy,' said a smiling American.

'He's got a good strong grip' I thought to myself. *(Dentists notice things like that.)*

Wendy continued the introduction, 'Bill is a Baptist Minister from New Jersey.'

'Yes,' replied Bill, 'and I've been having a lovely chat with your wife, hearing about your overland trip. It sounds like it's been a bit more rugged than this-here fancy tour my wife and I are doing.'

'Yes,' I replied smiling. 'It's had its moments.'

'So …' I asked Bill, 'how come you didn't go down into the catacombs with the rest of your group?'

'Well, it's like this. A couple of days ago, I had a fall and tore a ligament in my knee. Its working fine, a little painful, but mainly fine. If I stay on a path it's ok but it doesn't seem to like going up and down stairs.'

What followed was a wonderful hour of chatting together with someone who understood our faith and our situation, and when his wife returned with their group, we were introduced.

'Wendy and Graham, this is my wife Dorothy Jean.'

'Oh' replied Wendy 'Dorothy's my mother's name.'

There was an instant connection and we continued chatting.

Suddenly 'our Bill' began blowing the horn and the group started boarding the bus.

We thanked Bill and Dorothy Jean for the time we had spent with them, said our farewells, and began to walk back to our bus.

'Pardon me,' came Bill's voice from behind us.

We turned and he began walking towards us fumbling in his back pocket, Dorothy Jean by his side.

'Now' he continued 'I get the impression that you folks are in a little trouble and I suspect it might have something to do with your resources. *(How did he know?)* Have you run out of money?' he asked us point blank.

'No, no, no …' we protested weakly. 'We're fine.'

'Look' Bill said, ignoring our protestations and smiling knowingly, 'Would you prefer American dollars or Turkish Lira?'

'No, it's ok, seriously' we protested again. Not wanting to accept help – albeit foolishly.

'You'll be out of Turkey in a few days, so perhaps dollars would be better.' And with that, he opened his wallet, took out all the American dollars and thrust them into my hand.

'Sorry, it's not much but it will help I'm sure. It's all I have at the moment until we change more Travellers Cheques.'

'We can't take your money' we protested, holding the small wad of notes.

'It's not our money' Dorothy smiled 'it's the Lord's money' and with that they smiled and said, 'God bless you!'

'God bless you too,' we choked out, 'and thank you so much.'

With that we turned and ran to the bus. We were the last on and we clambered aboard, tears running down our cheeks. Nobody noticed. We resumed our seats. The bus pulled out and we just continued smiling at each other, wiping the tears away. And nobody noticed. God had just answered our groans, *(they weren't prayers, just groans)* and … nobody noticed. So bizarre. It was like we had a halo of light around us, but nobody noticed.

TURKISH DELIGHT

I opened my fingers. 'It's not much but it should help' Bill had said. There lay nineteen American dollars. We returned to Ürgüp with renewed thankfulness to God and greatly encouraged. It will surely help. We can make it with this.

From Ürgüp we travelled through central Turkey, passing through Konya, the home of the *whirling dervishes* but they only *whirl* on Wednesdays and Saturdays and it was Tuesday.

Bill decides to make a left turn and head for the coast again. We pass through thick pine forests, overshadowed by craggy outcrops of granite, deep valleys, mountain passes. Ahead of us the seaside town of Sidé – the thirteen-hour journey left us feeling like zombies, but the full day in Sidé, the following day, is very easy to take. An enjoyable walk through the old town, along the beach and round the headland, past Roman ruins, swimming in the sparkling azure waters of the Aegean Sea. A wonderful tonic for tiredness and depression. Hot showers, afternoon sleep. The stresses drift away but they'll be back we know.

We arrived at Ephesus to discover the entry fees were very expensive, but we weren't going to miss this historic site, (*even having to pay an extra fee for my camera*). So much Biblical history here – from the Acts of the Apostles, to Paul's Letter to the Ephesians, to the mention as one of the seven churches in Revelation. The ruins were excellent. Our budget suffered, but it was not to be missed.

A detour on the way to Istanbul gave us all a memorable and moving time at Gallipoli, the Lone Pine Memorial and Walkers Ridge, sites of some of the bloodiest battles of World War I for Australian and New Zealand troops.

Our impression driving into Istanbul is of grey concrete buildings, graffiti and painted slogans. The bus is headed for the *Poste Restante* and there were thirteen letters waiting for us. We found a little restaurant, a kind of pudding shop, and ordered some custard, to placate the owner. A wonderful hour and a half reading all those letters.

May 12th was a beautiful day in Istanbul to celebrate our third wedding anniversary. A return visit to the pudding shop, a wander through the bazaar and a visit to the beautiful Blue Mosque rounded off our tourist experience in Istanbul. A big box of Turkish Delight, a gift from two of the girls on the bus, a lovely anniversary gesture.

Two weeks in Turkey, sometimes wonderful, sometimes difficult, all dictated by the 'survival budget'. We really enjoyed the people and the country, but the 'God-moment' in Goreme was the unforgettable memory.

INTO EUROPE

Crossing into Greece, we set up camp in the seaside town of Kavalla. The beach is excellent, and the beautiful turquoise waters of the Mediterranean Sea a delight for swimming, the temperature of the water, perfect.

At this stage the 'kitty' for the evening meal is running low, so much of the time our diet has become either bread and tomatoes or bread and eggs, with the occasional 'gift' from our fellow travellers.

The routine that developed when we are camping in one place for more than one night, again plays out here. The 'party group' head into town early evening and return to camp around 2am very drunk and noisy. Often continuing the drinking and the noise well into the morning! We and a few others are beginning to tire of this routine … 'only ten days to London' we tell each other.

In Kavalla, we met a Christian girl called Anne from one of the other bus tours and spent many hours talking and sharing experiences. The final night in Kavalla, she gave us a farewell gift of a jar of strawberry jam, a tin of hot chocolate, and a packet of chocolate biscuits. Here too in Kavalla, there were tears of joy and rejoicing at the good news that our money had been recovered and was already in London waiting for us.

As we left Kavalla, we had good memories. This is the place called Neapolis in the Acts of the Apostles where Paul landed on his Second

Missionary journey and we have had some good Christian fellowship with Anne which greatly encouraged us.

From Kavalla we detoured to Philippi, another important town in the Early Church and the spread of Christianity. From my diary it seems I was also budgeting my photo-taking. *(This was the days of film with 36 exposures on a large roll.)* The diary records: 'I meant to only take one photo, but instead I took five'.

Also noted in my diary on the day we visited Thessalonika: 'Janet, one of our group, has asked to borrow our Bible and is reading about Paul's Missionary journeys in the Acts of the Apostles'.

Into the Old Yugoslavia and Skopje, the beautiful city situated on a river that was devastated by an earthquake in 1963. During the earthquake the railway station was partially demolished, and the clock stopped at 5.17am. It still stands as a silent memorial to the dead. Wandering along the picturesque path beside the river from the campsite to the town, there are young couples everywhere, hand in hand, strolling along the banks of the river. Very romantic, and still a strong memory to this day.

On the way back from dinner that night, we stumbled across a Yugoslav band – accordion, trumpet, trombone, and rhythm section. The music was fast, exciting, and compelling. I couldn't resist. I went up to the trumpeter during the break and with sign language, indicated I played trumpet. He handed me his trumpet, the band struck up *When the Saints go Marching in,* and I played along, really enjoying myself. The guitarist Atko, invited us to join him the next day but it was impossible as the bus was pushing on to Belgrade. This was one of the special nights of the trip.

The Yugoslav countryside is lush green and every piece of land possible is cultivated. There are lots of oxen ploughs in this rustic rural landscape rushing past our bus window. But soon the bus was slowing, and then stopped. We got a longer look at the countryside than we expected with a repair job that took almost two hours.

Belgrade was an impressive first sight. Towering office blocks, ancient buildings, beautiful streets, *and* a very nice Mo-camp.

It was our turn on the cook team that night. We were having trouble finding a supermarket or butcher's shop as nobody we met spoke English. Wendy solved the problem with a little role play, pretending to be first a cow (moo moo), then a sheep (baa baa), then gnawing on her arm. 'Oh yah, moo moo, baa baa' said a passer-by and pointed us in the right direction.

100 days from home and we're up early boiling water, cutting bread – our last duties as cooks. Leaving Belgrade, we notice the red poppies have disappeared and we now enter tall oak forests. Again, the scenery was changing, becoming even more picturesque, like model train villages. We arrived at Maribor, a quaint town, with narrow streets, looking out on a beautiful lake. The camping ground was alongside the lake, the ground very stony and it was hard to pitch our tents. Here it was discovered that Mike and others have been hiding the mallets in their tent bags to have them first, causing no little annoyance. We are all showing signs of stress.

Waking at 5am, we walked through the tiny village and surrounding pine forest. The scenery was superb, and we were engulfed in a warm glow as the sun rose over the mountain and instantaneously flooded the valley with its warmth.

We arrived at the Austrian border early, and it was then the charade began. The border guards approached the bus and walked past looking us up and down. No problems, we thought, or perhaps hoped; then suddenly the terse ultimatum, 'Everything out of the bus!' 'Oh, you are kidding' we all muttered as we picked up all the junk that had been accumulated over the previous weeks and piled it outside.

They searched our tents. They searched our suitcases. They searched the things on top of the bus. They searched the things in the belly of the bus. They planted marihuana *on* the bus and called in a sniffer dog who roamed the bus, finding the 'stash' and looking for other concealed drugs.

While this was happening, we wandered around and discovered a Bedford Dormobile, in excellent condition, also waiting to cross the border. We started up a conversation with the owners, an elderly couple, Mr and Mrs Chanel from Lockerbie in Scotland. They were on their last trip back to Mr Chanel's Eastern European country of birth, and then, they shared somewhat wistfully, they intended to sell the van.

As we drove into Austria, the dormobile was on our minds. We had taken their contact details and we'll see what happens when we reach London. But we just might buy it. Once we get money and can afford to buy anything more than bread and tomatoes.

The scenery in Austria becomes more and more Tyrolean, and we have the expectation of coming around a corner and running into Julie Andrews singing about how the hills are *alive* ...

Into Germany, with a stop at the salt mines, again too expensive for us to contemplate the tour. A walk instead, in the rain, shielded by trees, gazing over the valley, waiting for the bus.

Rick and Jude dropped into our tent later that day and *floored* us with 'we've accepted God's gift of eternal life.' Wendy and I couldn't believe what we were hearing and talked long into the evening about how and why and when and ... oh my goodness! Is this for real? Time will tell, like for me back in the Leigh College days.

On to Munich and Heidelberg. Constant rain. Wet tents – not easy to pitch or pack up. Freezing nights and more talking with Rick and Jude about the implications of their decision.

Sunday 23rd May, the final day and night of the trip. We were up early and ate the last of the cornflakes before pushing off on a long day covering 620 km. A really fun part of the journey that day when 'one of the Judys' revealed her little observations and favourite sayings of *everyone* on the bus.

Another revealing and amusing moment on that final day was when we pulled off the Autobahn at a roadhouse between Heidelberg and Bruges. Almost brain dead and pretty hungry at this stage, we bought some fruit and bread rolls for four Deutschmarks at the shop while the bus filled with fuel for the last leg. Then we entered the service station's restaurant wondering if we could afford anything. We bought one Bratwurst sausage and headed for a table to divide it between us.

Just as we made our way down past the numerous booths, a family of three slid out of their booth and headed for the exit. They left food ... on the table.

'Quick Wen. Before the waitress clears it away.'

There on the table was a bowl of salad, untouched, still covered with plastic, half a plate of chips (still warm) and half a glass of lemonade. We were very happy to augment our German sausage. Especially thankful to the three-year-old who hadn't eaten his lunch. It was delicious – we scoffed the lot! At this point, we have no shame.

INTO EUROPE

On to Brussels with its beautiful architecture, before heading to Bruges for the night. Our final evening meal, stale bread, augmented again with a German sausage.

Monday 24th May 1976, we crossed the English Channel by ferry and arrived in Southampton. We had less than three American dollars.

We spent it all on Mars Bars!

The drive to London went quickly and we were so pleased to be met by Bob and Chris Oliver and taken to their flat in Tufnell Park. Good friends, hot showers, and a warm bed! That first night, over a baked leg of lamb, roast potatoes and all the trimmings, we again marvelled at our 'divine intersection' – our incredible, unplanned, meeting with them, in church in Jerusalem, on Good Friday.

This flat, 91B Carleton Road, London N7, was to be our home until Wendy landed an unexpected job. But for now, we didn't care about what was ahead. We just cared that, after 106 days since leaving Sydney, *we had made it!*

THE CHURCH NEXT TO THE BBC

Most tourists, when they arrive in London, are off to see the sights but we had seen enough sites on the overland trip almost to last a lifetime, and so were happy just to settle into our flat in Tufnell Park.

Sunday arrived and we headed to church where we hoped to hear John Stott speak. *(We had heard him once before, in Australia, in an 'overflow tent' outside the main auditorium, at a missionary convention in Katoomba in 1975. It was a miserable day, drizzle and fog, the ground boggy, the TV picture grainy black and white, the disappointment high that we weren't inside the auditorium. However, his preaching on that chapter from Ephesians was so powerful, so genuine, so clear and well-reasoned, that it was worth it, despite the damp and cramped surroundings.)*

But when we arrived at 'All Souls Church Langham Place', next to the BBC at the top of Regent Street, it was closed.

A sign directed us to St Peter's Vere Street, several blocks away but the good news was the sermon board out the front of the boarded-up church told us John Stott was preaching at both morning and evening services today.

(The large congregation that attended every week had moved due to a major building project now in its second year. We arrived in the middle of this building project and the experience of being part of it, under the leadership of the Rector, Michael Baughen, was to have a major impact on our lives.)

But we didn't know that then ... we were just standing in the street looking at a sign saying a church was closed and where to find 'the hidden congregation'. We followed the directions and arrived a little late, finding a couple of cramped seats at the back of the church behind a column with a limited view of the pulpit, craning our necks, Wendy one way and me the other. Michael Baughen, leading the service and giving an update on the state of the building project, exhorted us all to 'mean business with the living God' and added, 'it was not *our* great faith in God, but faith in a great God' that would see the church re-opened later that year free of debt. Then he introduced the speaker we had come to hear, the Rector Emeritus, John Stott, who, he explained, had just returned from speaking overseas. A very humble man entered the pulpit and we and the rest of the multi-cultural congregation fell silent.

(John Stott, increasingly invited to speak and teach around the world, had asked Michael Baughen in 1970 to consider taking over the leadership role at All Souls freeing him for this mushrooming global ministry of preaching, teaching, and writing. John would become 'Rector Emeritus' and maintain his close connection with the church of his childhood for the rest of his life.)

It was an arrangement that worked beautifully for the ministries of All Souls and John Stott's 'Langham Trust' *(which morphed, in later years, into 'The Langham Partnership')*. Michael Baughen, married to Myrtle, was a family man, and complemented the ministry of John who, though he never married, had a 'family' who loved him spread across the globe and called him 'Uncle John'.

John Stott was incredibly gifted, a double first in Theology and Languages at Cambridge. And apart from his preaching and teaching, his founding role in the 'Lausanne Movement', along with numerous other organisations which he pioneered or influenced, he was a Chaplain to the Queen; and by the end of his life had written more than 50 books. In 2005 he was voted one of the top 100 most influential people of the twentieth century by *Time* magazine.

His first book, *Basic Christianity*, sold in the millions but all the profits from this and his many other books were channelled into strengthening the Church in what he called the 'Majority World', through the Langham Trust. *(Basic Christianity was one of the main influences in my decision to become a Christian.)*

THE CHURCH NEXT TO THE BBC

All Souls was an amazing church that we loved from the first moment. It was 'packed to the rafters' every service, with over a thousand enthusiastic members of the congregation singing their hearts out. The preaching was the best we had ever heard. The people were friendly and welcoming. The congregation had members and visitors from countries all round the world and a huge student population. And, for Wendy and me, both musicians (violin and trumpet), the music was unbelievable and a very important part of the church's ministry. Michael Baughen, a gifted musician and composer, had with others, pioneered 'Youth Praise' which revolutionised praise and worship amongst young people round the world. He also had appointed a talented young man called Noël Tredinnick to be the church's musical director and together with Noël had launched 'Psalm Praise' which gave the psalms a new and contemporary feel. *(Noel was to have a major impact on Christian music over the next five decades.)*

The first time we heard the orchestra play back in St Peter's Vere Street, Lesley Sidey, a young female trumpeter, played the Third Movement of Hummel's Trumpet Concerto. I had never heard anything like this in church before and, as a trumpeter myself, I was transfixed. The hairs on the back of my neck were standing up as she played the technically difficult triplet section towards the end of the piece without a note out of place.

After that service, I asked Noël if there was room for another trumpeter (brash Aussie that I was) and was informed politely they had enough trumpets at the time but, hearing Wendy played violin and viola, immediately conscripted her to play in the viola section. *(Which she did and really enjoyed, especially the time the orchestra backed Cliff Richard.)* Meanwhile, I had to bide my time on the 'sidelines'. My opportunity to play in the orchestra came in 1977 when the National Evangelical Anglican Congress was held in Nottingham and Lesley's second trumpet couldn't do 'the gig'. So, I got to play alongside her and we became friends, sharing many a laugh from the back row. I was absorbed into the orchestra from then on and both Wendy and I enjoyed being a part of that music ministry up until the time we left London to return home.

At that first service we attended in St Peter's Vere Street (sitting behind pillars with limited visibility like I said), it was announced John Stott would be leading the student bible study the following Friday morning.

He was doing a series on the deepest of New Testament books, Paul's Letter to the Romans, chapters five to eight. This series was absolute gold for keen young Christians wanting their faith to grow. The only negative was it began at 6am. *We decided to set the alarm.*

We were first to arrive, and John Stott was the second! Oh, my goodness. It was to us, like meeting royalty. But his friendliness immediately disarmed us and put us at ease. Well, not exactly at ease. He was genuinely interested in us, asking of our travels, as we were let into the meeting room. Looking for something to say, I blurted out, 'We were the only Christians on the bus. I wish I was able to argue the Christian faith better'. 'My dear brother' (I can hear his gentle voice now), 'you don't win people into the kingdom by *arguing*, you win them by *loving* them'.

We found our seats with me feeling like I had put my foot in it, my face flushed. But it wasn't a put-down, it was the godliest man we have ever met encouraging us in *genuine* sharing of the Christian gospel. *(I still remember that moment, 45 years later and 'Uncle John' was to become a dear friend of us both.)*

The moment passed as others arrived. His humility and intellect lit up this group of keen Christians and genuine searchers. It was a privilege to be there.

The Student Pastor organising this group was a young American, Greg Scharf, married to Ruth**,** an English girl. We continued attending the student group and in the course of time, the friendship grew and one day, Ruth discovered Wendy was a 'fashion teacher'.

'Fashion? Do you mean dressmaking?' asked Ruth, 'I am having a problem with a dress-making project, a bridesmaid's dress, and the wedding is not far away.'

It was that conversation that changed our plans about returning to Australia.

In fact, it changed everything really.

On our arrival in London, Wendy, unable to teach, had re-trained as a secretary receptionist and at the end of training, found a job in central London at film and theatre production company Mitchell, Monkhouse & Associates (MMA), working with Denis Norden, Frank Muir and other comedians, fielding calls from Morecambe and Wise, and David

Frost, all celebrities of radio and TV at the time – quite an experience for a young Aussie girl.

Wendy's 'fashion' skills were called on again some months later when, in the final stages of the building project, Michael Baughen asked the staff meeting, if anyone knew *someone* who could design and produce 60 choir robes to match the new interior colour scheme of the church. But there was a deadline – the reopening of the church was scheduled for the 2nd of November 1976, only two months away.

Greg Scharf mentioned there was an Australian girl in the congregation who'd helped his wife, and maybe they could ask her. Noël Tredinnick, the Musical Director would contact Wendy. They met. Wendy designed the robes and assembled a team of church ladies ready and willing to produce this mountain of choir robes within the time. An enormous task, given they all had day jobs.

Although working full time at MMA, from 5pm till 2am for the 6 weeks prior to the opening, Wendy and her indefatigable team of helpers would assemble in the vestry of All Souls, and after a little friendly banter, get down to some serious measuring, cutting, and sewing rolls and rolls of material. I was an onlooker, organising food for the group, reading, and often falling asleep in a chair or stretched out on the floor. They'd wake me when they needed a cup of tea or coffee. Out of that working group developed strong friendships that have stood the test of time. *(They finished the robes on schedule.)*

Under the leadership of Michael Baughen, ever reliant on the ability of God to provide the funds needed, the church re-opened on All Souls Day, the 2nd of November 1976, free of debt. There was a line of people stretching down Regent Street and not everyone could fit in the church.

Wendy and I, having been part of the 'choir robe team', had seats in the front row of the upper right-hand gallery looking down on the sixty-piece orchestra, along with the choir, resplendent in their new robes.

During the making of the choir robes, Michael Baughen was watching this young Aussie girl work with what seemed like endless amounts of goodwill, pro-activity, and energy. He asked her if she would be his personal assistant, as his present assistant was soon to marry and move out of London. This meant staying longer in London, but it was an opportunity we couldn't miss. Wendy eagerly took the job!

SEMI-FINAL AND FINALE

Working for Michael Baughen, together with John Stott and alongside his delightful and omni-competent personal assistant Frances Whitehead, was one of the greatest privileges of Wendy's life. Living in one of the two small flats at the back of the church, with a car parking space in central London, was an amazing experience for both of us. We got to see the 'workings' of the church and the people 'up close', and we were not disappointed.

We were astounded to find the All Souls prayer gathering, the fortnightly Tuesday night meeting where the 'church family' came together, drawing several hundred people. Prayer meetings typically were half a dozen of the most committed, but this was obviously the 'engine room' of the church, and not to be missed. But it wasn't all serious and we were surprised at John Stott's dry wit and sense of humour that he shared with the prayer gathering from time to time.

In a big church like All Souls, it was easy to think 'there is no room for a couple of Aussies to do anything' but, after we had been there only a few months attending services and that amazing prayer meeting, they announced the need for youth leaders for the 'Pathfinder' group (twelve to fifteen-year-olds). We enquired and found that another Aussie couple were also interested – Bill and Robyn Hawkshaw. We were all accepted (after interviews) and joined Judith Chapman in the leadership team. This was a great time and a great group of young kids. There were many wonderful discussions and outings together, but the camp in the Cotswolds is a special memory.

(One of the Pathfinders we mentored, Toby Howarth, was fifteen years old when we left the UK to return home, Wendy pregnant with Matthew. Twenty years later, Matthew and Toby found themselves in the same city in the Subcontinent doing research, and then it was Toby's turn to mentor Matthew. Isn't life strange?)

One thing I had wrestled with over the years after becoming a Christian was, 'Does this mean I should now become a pastor and give up dentistry?' One of John Stott's main emphases I heard in our time at All Souls was the 'training of the laity for works of service' – 'service' in the place God has put you.

During our first year in London, I became disillusioned with the 'dentistry factory' approach of the practice where I was working. The 'boss' constantly pushed everyone to make bigger weekly totals which invariably meant working faster and 'cutting corners'. I found that it was impossible to treat patients as people, they were just teeth that walked in and opportunities to make as much money as the National Health System would allow. A patient arrived in my chair with their treatment plan from the boss – 'a crown on the lower left first molar'. I looked in the mouth and found a small hole in that tooth, so I did the most conservative restoration I could, which was not a crown. A crown brought in fifteen times more income than the humble filling; and my bottom line was, the crown wasn't warranted. But the boss' philosophy was to maximise profit, and our 'bottom lines' didn't match up. I left that practice not long afterwards.

Because I was again wrestling with the whole issue of what to do with my life and my skills and should I go into 'ministry'. Greg Scharf advised me to use this opportunity between dental jobs to do the one-year 'Bible and Mission' course at London Bible College (LBC). Not only was it 'helpful' and inspiring, but God knew what was ahead!

During the time we were at All Souls, Greg Scharf appointed three 'lay student pastors' – John Wyatt, who was a young doctor; David Turner, a young lawyer; and to my amazement, a young dentist. After the year at LBC and with what I heard from the All Souls' pulpit, especially from John Stott's preaching and teaching; alongside the student work with Greg, John and David, I began to see that as a dentist I could have many different opportunities to serve.

Living 'above the office', Wendy would often work extra hours to *finish* a task. One of the church wardens, offered us their little cottage in the countryside for a few days break. The 'little cottage' in the picturesque village of Inkpen was a centuries-old building with a thatched roof and oak beams that could have been on a postcard. Winding leafy lanes, paddocks with cows listlessly chewing their cud, hedgerows, blackbirds singing in the dead of night. What could be more restful? We wandered the lanes, ate ploughman's lunches at the local pub, read the books that we had been intending to open for months. Idyllic. But I became restless. The reason ... it was the second week of Wimbledon. It was the semi-finals, John McEnroe v Jimmy Connors, and Vitas Gerulaitis v Björn Borg.

I convinced Wendy we should leave our leafy paradise and head for SW20. The place was packed. We paid at the gate and entered the swirl of humanity, pushing and shoving in a gentlemanly and womanly fashion towards Centre Court. We had no tickets. But at Centre Court, I had researched, they had 'standing room only'. We found and joined the queue. So many people ahead of us, in a line that never seemed to end, edging towards an entrance *under* the stands. The game began. We are outside the stadium and can hear the roar of the crowd at each point.

With 'standing room only', the officials only allow one person to enter as one person leaves. But people don't want to leave this semi-final, with the superstars slugging it out in magnificent fashion, and so, we are left 'out in the cold' under a burning sun. Eventually we're in the cement tunnel, under the stands where people are sitting in comfort watching the battle unfold. All we can see are the backs of irritated people's heads and a concrete enclosure bearing in on us as the minutes become hours.

It's like hell, I thought, here we are, we can hear the crowd inside, but we can't get there. We are excluded. In the tunnel. We're enclosed in concrete with people we don't know and who aren't happy about the situation and who are voicing their annoyance incessantly and we are forbidden entry to the hallowed ground where everyone is having such a good time!

I need the loo. 'Mind my place', I say to Wendy. I leave the queue and push my way back through the 'sardine can' and find the toilets. *At least they are not blocked.*

As I leave the men's room, I spy a door labelled 'Ground Staff Only' and there's no guard on the door. I wonder … I wonder if I could get a glimpse of the game through that door. I look around. No guard, no officials. So, with my heart in my mouth, I walk towards the door and grasp the handle, looking like this is an everyday occurrence for me, I am meant to be here, doing this. It's unlocked. I slip through. It's a sort of large storage room, open at one end. Blinding light, noise, thumps as a tennis ball is served at 200 kph. There are one or two people standing round at the end looking towards the noise, and there's a large roller with someone standing on it, watching the action. I climb up beside him, nodding in greeting as if I am meant to be there. A few short metres from me, is Jimmy Connors, smashing a double-handed back hand return, down the line for a winner. At the other end, John McEnroe is 'chucking' a tantrum. This is great! Its halfway through the third set and the tide has turned. McEnroe is gaining the ascendancy. And no-one has noticed me, no-one cares that I am standing on that huge roller watching the tennis match of my life only a few metres behind Connors!

They change ends and suddenly, I remember Wendy, with 'tunnel vision', watching the wall. I dismount from the roller and nodding to the others, take my leave.

We didn't get to see Connors take the next set and the match, but we could hear the screams of celebration … and we weren't part of it. Yes, the 'exclusion' I reflected.

Enough people left the 'standing room' between games to enable us to enter. We had made it, Centre Court, and here come the players for the second semi-final. Björn Borg! (Cheering!) Vitas Gerulaitis! (More cheering!) They began their 'hit-up'. It was a long match. Björn won in five sets and went on to beat Connors in the *Men's Final* two days later.

As we are leaving, we passed 'the door'. There is now a guard standing there. We found our car and returned late to the leafy lanes of Inkpen.

SEMI-FINAL AND FINALE

All good things come to an end. Our time at All Souls, two and a half years, was one of the most influential periods of our lives. Towards the end of 1978, with Wendy 'expecting' our first child, we decided it was time to go home. The farewell from Michael, the staff team, and friends, was very special and the beautiful clock they gave us is still telling us the time and reminding us of *that time*.

We had come to England overland by bus, and we returned to Australia by sea. Sailing from Southampton via Bermuda, through the Panama Canal, and north to Vancouver. In Vancouver, the boat picked up a family called 'Boys', also returning from a significant time living away from Australia. We both had made the decision a 'slow' return was a good way to begin the 'transition'! Ron and Robyn had three boys and were expecting another. With Wendy and Robyn in a 'similar state', we gravitated together and became friends for the rest of the cruise and, in fact, to this day.

From Vancouver, we sailed to Hawaii, arriving in *Pearl Harbour* on the anniversary of the World War Two attack. Then on to Fiji, Auckland and finally entering Sydney Harbour. With excitement rising, we berthed at Circular Quay. It was so good to see the Harbour Bridge and the Opera House ... and to be back home.

Family and friends were waiting and, after a voyage of forty days and forty nights on a boat, much more comfortable than the Biblical one, we disembarked to begin life again in Australia.

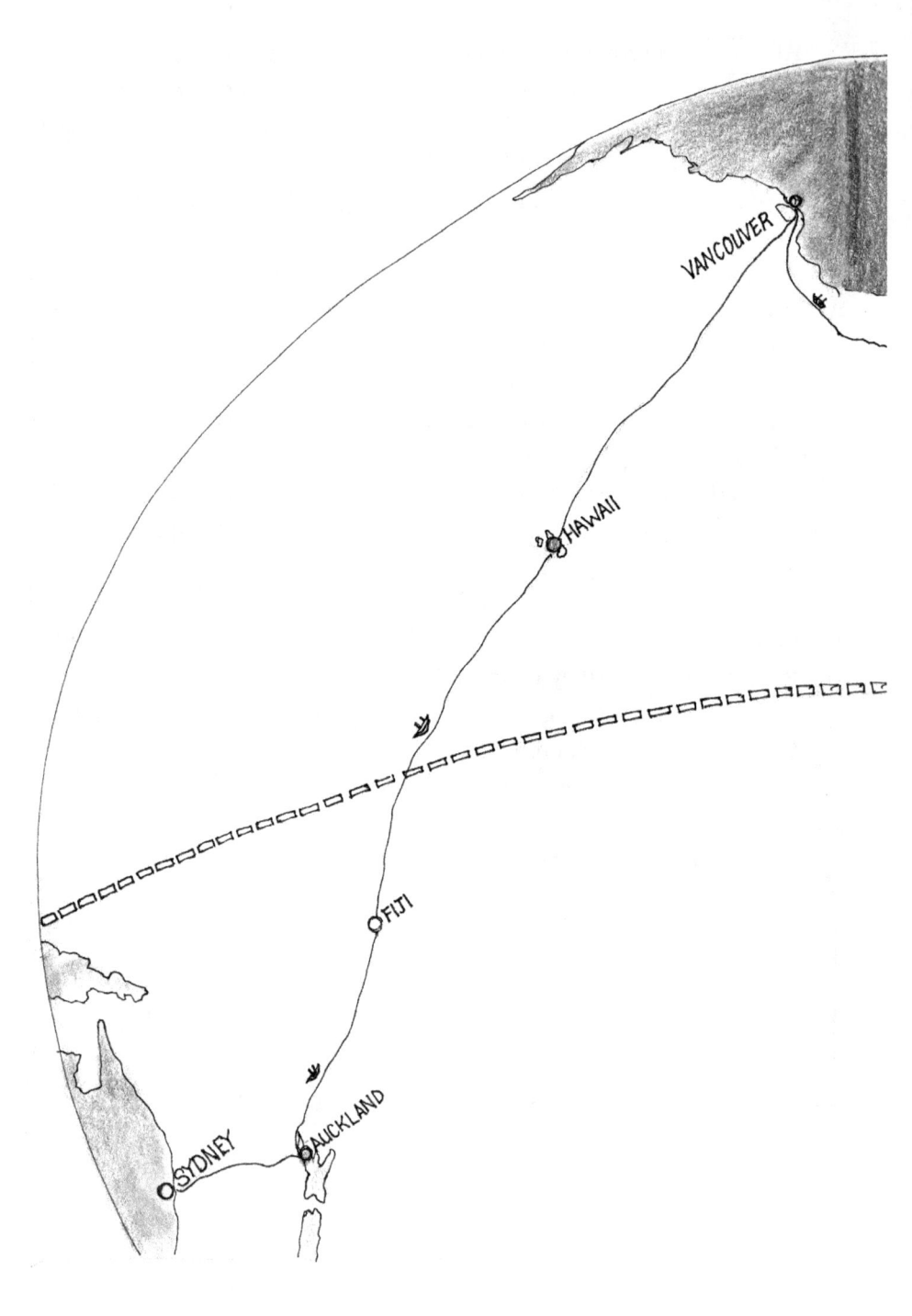

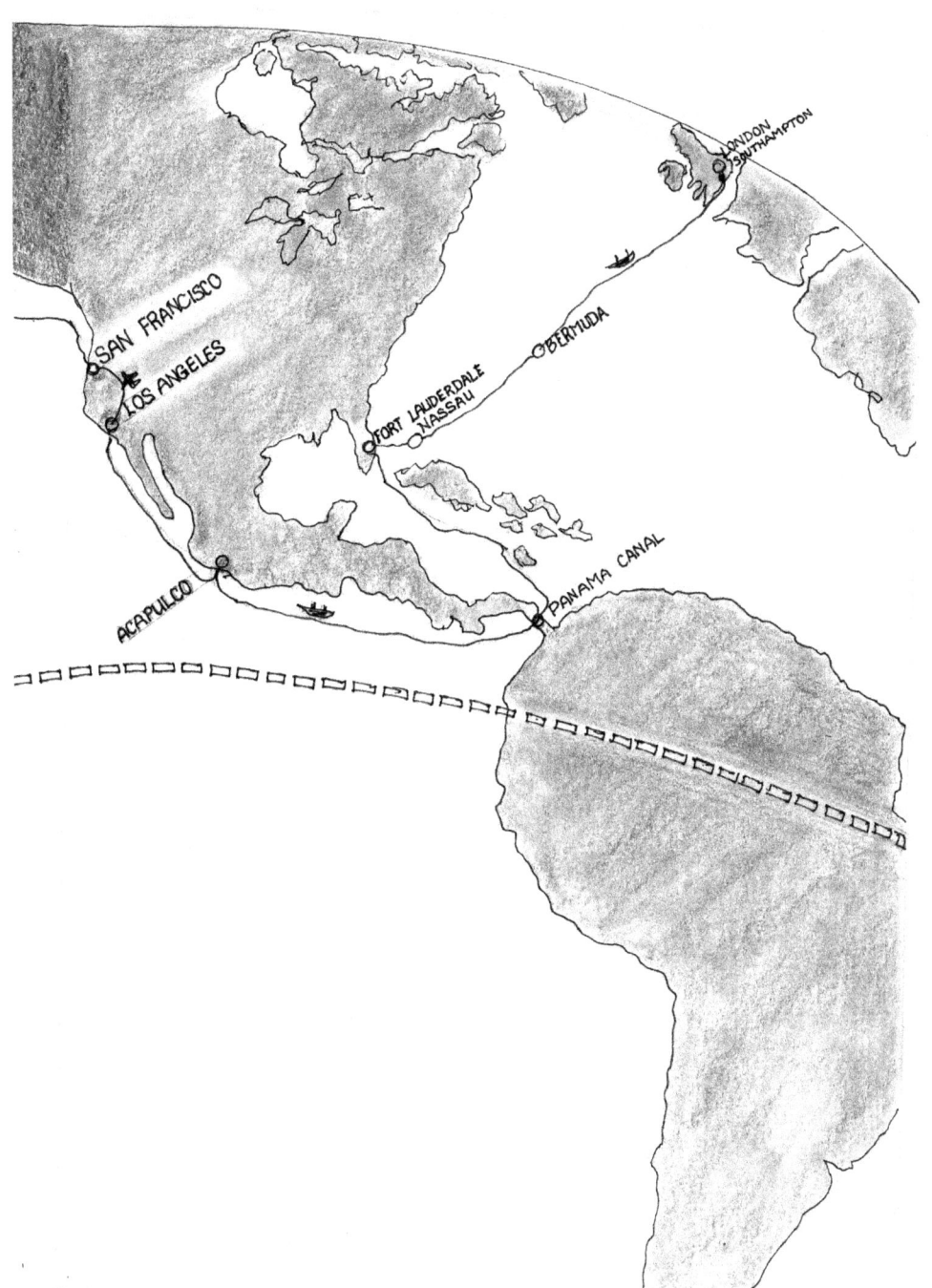

FORK IN THE ROAD

BABIES AND BATONS

We had come home with nothing and needed a place to live, a place to work, and an obstetrician. I was able to find work in Parramatta, not far from where we were renting an apartment. Wendy found part-time work and began preparing for the coming family.

We had become settled (Peter Boase's words were slowly becoming a distant memory). We bought a house in the Blue Mountains outside of Sydney and found a church there. Wendy and I again were involved in youth work at the church, and I started an 'Agnostics Anonymous' group modelled on our All Souls' experience, sharing the leadership with Bob Johnston, the Headmaster of the John Wycliffe Christian School. I remembered John Stott's words and tried to apply them in this discussion group. With all the members being agnostic or atheist except for Bob and me, the discussion became, at times, quite robust with some members really challenging our beliefs *(as I had done with Rob Forsyth)* and we, in turn, challenging theirs. Sharing and defending our Christian faith was, at times, a bit like getting a migraine for fun, but we remained friends and some of them, to our surprise, changed their 'world views' over the course of several years. This, I thought, was 'my mission'. I had no thoughts of 'heading overseas'.

I spent two years working in Parramatta and then, with our move to the mountains and the commute to work each day, was challenged by a friend, Rex Lamb, to open my own dental surgery in Springwood. He rang one day saying the local paper was advertising some 'rooms to rent' with a local doctor and encouraged me to 'give it a go'.

Dr Warwick Beddoes had two spare rooms, and with a certain amount of trepidation, I took the 'plunge', rented those rooms, leased some dental equipment and my career as a suburban dentist took off. The patient load over the next eighteen months exploded and so I moved into larger premises. Not long after, my old friend from student days, Roger Phillips, joined me and a year or two later, we bought our own premises. Life was good. I was establishing my dental practice and we were paying the bills. Wendy was involved in motherhood, church activities and part-time work. By this time, we had three very active boys, Matthew, Michael, and Stephen, who kept us occupied in many ways … and, oh I forgot to mention, we had become part of the music ministry at a missionary conference held each year in the Blue Mountains. It came about in this way …

In 1979, while we were still trying to find our feet back in Australia and before we had bought a house or started a dental practice, we were delighted to hear that Michael Baughen, from All Souls, was coming to Australia to speak at a conference and was bringing musical director, Noël Tredinnick, with him. The conference was the weeklong 'Summer School' for the Church Missionary Society (CMS) of the Anglican Church, held early January each year in Katoomba in the Blue Mountains, only 30 km from where we bought our house. *(This was the same conference where we first heard John Stott speak in 1975.)*

Noël contacted us and asked if we could organise a small orchestra to accompany the singing for the conference. This was the way Wendy and I became involved in Summer School, through an interest and commitment to the music ministry, it wasn't because of an interest in overseas mission.

Michael spoke each morning with Noël conducting the orchestra for the singing and we had a rollicking good time. So much so that the following year, with no Noël, Wendy was asked if she would take up the baton!

Each morning of the conference the keynote speaker would address the packed auditorium in the first session, book-ended with singing, then would come the tea and coffee break. After morning tea, the second session would begin where the CMS missionaries would talk about their work, their lives in another culture, their joys, and difficulties.

Now I must be brutally honest. At this point in my life, in the early eighties, I thought we had our life-plan worked out. I had my own dental practice in Springwood, Wendy was busy with family life, her part-time teaching-work, we were involved in music at church and Summer School, and we were parents, producing progeny at a regular rate. I didn't want any changes to our settled lifestyle now that we were established in the Blue Mountains community. I had little interest in anything to do with missionaries and their lives.

So instead of going to the missionary sessions, Wendy and I went into the village of Katoomba and drank coffee and chatted with our friends Robert and Lesley Scott. We had met this couple in rather unusual circumstances in 1977 during our 'London detour'.

While travelling in our Bedford Dormobile (the one we saw at the Yugoslav Austrian border and bought in Scotland), we arrived in Paris and found a camping spot in the Bois de Boulogne. There were campervans and tents everywhere but the campervan right behind ours, had some familiar stickers on the back window – an Australian flag and a fish symbol. A young couple obviously 'doing Europe' emerged from the van.

We smiled. They smiled back.

'Gidday'

We then asked the obvious question.

'Are you Aussies?'

'Yes', they replied in a familiar accent.

'Are you Christians?' (the fish symbol was a giveaway).

'Yes, we are', came the reply.

'Where do you go to church?' was my next question.

'Carlingford Presbyterian', they replied.

'You don't! ... Really? ... We are from Epping Presbyterian.'

(Carlingford and Epping are adjoining suburbs in Sydney.)

After that, the conversation continued and to our surprise, we discovered we had been singing Christmas carols on the back of the same truck the year before we had left Australia. A seriously amazing coincidence, we all agreed. That was the start of a long and ongoing friendship.

This 'tradition' with Rob and Les continued for five years. Orchestra playing, the CMS crowd singing, Wendy conducting, main speaker speaking … then off for coffee and a chat while the missionary sessions took place. Evening sessions were singing and a focus on mission somewhere in the world. It was impossible to avoid these evening sessions being in the orchestra.

Then came the Sunday night session of 1985.

THE CMS STORY BEGINS

That Sunday night meeting at Summer School 1985 began normally with singing and then a CMS staff member, the Reverend Peter Dawson, was introduced. He had just returned from an exploratory visit to Zaïre with another CMS staffer, Ross Hall. As a result of increasing requests from the two Anglican Bishops on the eastern side of this impoverished central African country, CMS had sent these two to 'spy out the land'. Peter had put together a slideshow to promote the formation of the 'Z Team', a group of missionaries they hoped to gather to go and help the Anglican Church in Zaïre with Theological Education, Health and Technical needs.

There was no mention of the need for a dentist. Doctors, yes, but nothing about my profession. Some of the slides that flashed on the screen resonated with me, being very similar to the Papua New Guinea highlands Wendy and I had visited more than ten years earlier.

I wasn't expecting to be challenged. This was just part of the evening and I was there as a musician. That's all.

Hmmm, that's interesting I thought. Looks like a place full of adventures, bit like PNG. Terrible roads though, my thoughts continuing.

Then the voice-over said:

'A knowledge of French, though not essential, would be a great help.'

I remember thinking … Well French was my best subject at high school but … *(and then my defence mechanisms came into play)* … that was 20 years ago … and, for that matter, I'm not really interested in going to Africa … and certainly not long term. No way!

Besides, I rationalised, I have a dental practice in Springwood and three children and to think about 'selling-up' would be irresponsible and the disruption, unthinkable. So, I dismissed the whole invitation or challenge as something for somebody else to consider.

The week passed uneventfully until Friday morning.

It was customary for CMS to have an 'Enquirers' Meeting' last thing on the Friday morning before the conference 'wound up', for those who might seriously be thinking about 'going'. I found myself there in that meeting, not out of interest but to encourage someone else to think about that process of 'going'.

The speaker, Peter Tasker, the NSW General Secretary at the time, was telling those present the necessary steps to be accepted as a CMS missionary. *(It was pretty rigorous I remember thinking.)*

He explained that before even a discussion of 'going' could take place, the candidates would need to have done, at least, a year of Bible College training or preferably a three-year theological degree.

(Well, I thought, I did a year at London Bible College during our time in England, but fortunately what he is saying is for my friend alongside.)

Then the candidates would apply to CMS, be interviewed, and psychologically assessed, and if accepted, undergo, at their own expense, a cross-cultural training regime of five months living in community at St Andrews Hall in Parkville, Melbourne.

*(This would mean selling the practice **before** being accepted – are you serious? Well, that's not going to happen, I continued thinking. Why am I thinking this anyway, this doesn't apply to me?)*

During this time in Melbourne, Peter continued, there would be multiple interviews by individuals and committees to assess if the candidates had 'what it took' to work cross-culturally and *survive* in the often-difficult places where they were being sent. Then finally, when candidates were accepted, there was an extended time of language learning, often in the country to which you were being sent. CMS required a commitment of at least six years, two three-year terms with a six-month home assignment in between.

I was doing the calculations while he spoke and with our oldest son, Matthew, six years old, the preparation and training and then the six years, he would be in his mid-teens, and that would be the time to come back to re-establish him in high school in Australia. My mind was racing. If this mind-boggling, life-changing, crazy idea was going to happen … Wendy and I had to act *now*.

I left the meeting confused. 'Was that an emotional meeting?' I asked a clergy friend, Lloyd Bennett. 'Not a bit' he replied, 'it was just the nuts and bolts of what you have to do to apply and be accepted'. 'Well, I was really moved' I countered. 'Look,' he said, 'go away and try to forget all about it and if the thought is still there after a month, go and talk to someone at CMS'.

Still confused, I headed down the hill to meet Wendy who had picked up the kids from their morning program. She saw the confused look on my face and asked what was wrong.

'Nothing' I replied, 'except I think we might be going to Africa.'

'OK' she said confidently, as if I had said we were off to do some shopping, and we headed to the carpark with our three young boys not knowing that our life together had just changed direction.

The trip home from that 1985 CMS Summer School was longer than usual with holiday traffic choking the Great Western Highway. The three boys chatted and laughed and teased each other and giggled and whinged – the usual road trip with a family – but, apart from settling minor disputes in the back seat, Wendy and I were both deep in thought. The seriousness of my throw-away line – 'we might be going to Africa' – was sinking in; and going through my mind, as I drove down the mountain from Katoomba, were all sorts of unanswerable questions. No doubt it was the same for Wendy, but she hadn't been at that Enquirers' Meeting and I had a lot of 'unpacking' of what I had heard and what this decision might mean for us as a family.

I was watching the road, but I wasn't seeing the villages as we passed through them. Leura, Wentworth Falls, Bullaburra, Lawson, Hazelbrook, Woodford, Linden – were all a blur. Faulconbridge, and I came to, so to speak. Nearly home. The boy's noise continued as we unloaded them in front of our little house in Coomassie Avenue. Wendy and I had lots to discuss, but for now the 'family duties' took over as the boys ran into the house.

That night, after the kids were all settled in bed, we began talking. My unwillingness to even contemplate 'being a missionary in Africa' had somehow evaporated. I relayed all the information Peter Tasker had shared, what we would have to do in the coming months, if we decided to proceed. We laughed over the strange fact that when we first started attending Summer School in January 1980, there was a dear elderly returned-missionary lady we met, called Beryl. When she found out I was a dentist, her eyes lit up as she exclaimed, 'They need dentists in Tanzania, in Dodoma where I worked!' to which I lamely replied 'Oh, really?' and changed the subject. Every year after that she would say 'I'm praying for you to go to Tanzania.' And every year my response was the same lame 'Oh, really?'

'Funny, isn't it?' I said to Wendy that night, 'Zaïre and not Tanzania. I wonder what Beryl will say?'

A month went by, the same thoughts were going through our heads, so we made that appointment with Peter Tasker and began the long process of interviews, questionnaires, medicals etc, etc, etc. There were plenty of problems to work through.

What should we do with the dental practice? What will my parents say when I tell them I am selling-up and going to Africa? What about moving a young family to Africa – is that a wise thing to do? What about sickness? What about the boys' education? What about leaving family and friends … Dad is not well, should I leave?

We continued talking and working through the problems one by one.

DON'T GIVE UP ON US

During the years Wendy led the singing at Summer School, we had the privilege of staying in 'Speaker's Lodge' at the Katoomba Christian Convention site where CMS staff and their families, together with the speakers were all accommodated. It made sense for Wendy, needing to organise two rehearsals for the orchestra each day, to stay on site. And where Wendy went, the rest of us tagged along. It was great for our whole family. The homely atmosphere and so many young girls who would babysit and 'mother' each of our children as they came along in those years from 1980 to 1986. During the years we stayed in Speaker's Lodge, we got to know the CMS staff well, and each year met the guest speakers. (We will never forget Elisabeth Elliot entertaining us all one night after the evening session on the piano, as well as wonderful conversations with others like John White and Michael Griffiths – special memories.)

It was during this time we met and became good friends with Howard and Glenda Whitehouse. At that time, Howard was the manager of the CMS Book Shops and it was Glenda who later became our 'prayer letter' secretary – photocopying and posting out hundreds of *'Touligrams'!*

Early 1985, we were invited to the home of Terry and Beverley Cox. (Beverley was one of my dental nurses and Terry was a sound engineer.) With their good friend, Lionel Murray, they had bought a five-acre block in Queens Road, Lawson, and had established 'Windwood Studios'.

During the meal, the conversation turned to the recording studio and after dinner Terry took me to have a look at the 'set-up'. He had invited me to bring my trumpet that night and, in the studio, got me to 'play along' to a backing track. It didn't sound too bad. My brain started whirring.

'Hey Wen ... what do you think about making a cassette recording and giving it to our parents for Christmas. My Mum would love hearing me play a bit of trumpet when we are away overseas.'

I discussed the idea with Howard, and he thought it might have wider appeal – 'it just might have legs'. He agreed to help us as he had experience in musical promotion with some rather well-known Christian artists in the past, so had the background knowledge that I didn't on production and promotion. 'Let's hear what you can do' he challenged me, and with that encouragement, I was off and running.

I approached family and friends, (who were musicians) and, over a period of several months, we recorded twelve songs producing a cassette master tape with a variety of musical styles – Classical, Christian, and Popular. I wanted the recording to be a 'family affair' so Wendy was on violin, I was on trumpet and we wanted the kids to do a track as well. (Well not Steve as he had only just been born and hadn't realised his musical ability at that early stage.)

Then there was Wendy's family. Her mother was a competent violinist, so that's two in our string section. Her father had a beautiful bass voice, so he was in the 'choir'. Wendy's eldest sister, Pamela, a classical piano teacher – yes, I thought, we can definitely do a couple of little trumpet voluntaries with Pamela accompanying me. Then the other sisters, Julie, a great voice, also plays cello, (we can use that). Cathy, the youngest sister, not easy to incorporate her trumpet talent, as she was living in New Zealand!

On my side of the family, Mum had been a good violinist in her day, touring with a group organized by her father in the Depression, doing concerts around New South Wales prisons, to lift people's spirits during that hard time, but she graciously declined, saying, 'she was not the violinist she used to be'. Dad was in poor health and his piano playing abilities were limited. In our childhood, he would occasionally be encouraged to play the one classical piece he had learnt note by note, a piece by Paderewski. My sister had foolishly given up her piano career in her primary school days and pursued ballroom dancing, and my older brother was in America. Friends Robert and Lesley Scott got dragged in as well for some piano and backing vocals, their boys, Paul six and Steve four, joined our two boys of the same ages, Matthew and Michael.

Next, I got talking to friends, Glen and Kerry McCaffery, who were in a band called 'Witness' and the group agreed to do three tracks including the title track – 'Don't Give Up on Me'.

Then I ran into a mate, John Robertson, who had a great voice, and he agreed to do two tracks, including the final song that would bring a lump to the throat, and a tear to the eye, of any Australian overseas, 'I still call Australia Home'.

Terry Cox held the reins at the sound desk, and drank a lot of Coke, his partner, Lionel Murray, contributing some flamboyant flute tracks.

Behind it all, was the Executive Producer, Howard Whitehouse who had the bright idea of producing a number of these cassettes and selling them in the CMS bookshops once we were accepted as CMS missionary candidates. We called it 'Don't give up on us' after the title track with the idea that the music would remind the listener to pray for us while we were training in Melbourne and then later serving in Africa.

But what to do with the dental practice? The one-man dental practice was a difficult one. We can't leave the practice vacant for our five months training in Melbourne – which means we must sell. But, if we sell and it doesn't work out in Melbourne, or we are rejected by CMS as not suitable for mission work, what do we do then? We have burnt our bridges. We came to the conclusion we had to step out in faith, we believed God was in this whole process and so we put the dental practice on the market.

In six months, not one person showed interest in buying. We had no idea, as we began to advertise the practice in dental circles mid-year, that the person who would eventually buy it, wasn't even in the country. He and his wife returned from England in the December, asked Michael Payne, from the Christian Dental Fellowship, if he knew of any practices for sale. They contacted us, and it was all settled by the end of the year. We had endured months of waiting and fretting and then came the final resolution that had our heads spinning. We were now free of that responsibility.

Just before Christmas of that year, 1985, our fourth son Jeremy was born, our family now complete. Then in late January the following year, Wendy and I packed our four boys into the Nissan Urvan and began the 900 km journey to Melbourne and the five months cross-cultural training at St. Andrew's Hall. With three active boys and a newborn, we knew it was not going to be easy.

THE ROAD TO MELBOURNE

After twelve hot and sticky, long and difficult hours on the Hume Highway, heading south, with frequent stops for crying children, food or rest breaks, we pulled into the driveway of 190 The Avenue Parkville, Melbourne, thoroughly exhausted.

Immediately we were overwhelmed by people wanting to help us unpack and settle in. We were welcomed by the Principal, John MacIntosh and his wife Barbara, and the Deputy Principal Margaret Lawry along with the other 'missionary candidates' and their children.

St Andrews Hall
Parkville

At that time, in 1986, the beautiful old home became known to all of us as 'The White House'. This is where all the lectures took place and where we had the community meals at lunch and dinner. That year, our training group consisted of eighteen adults and seventeen children (and a possum) all housed in a three-story cement-block accommodation building at the back of the property, separated from 'The White House' by a back yard dominated by a huge centrally placed willow tree, perfect for children's climbing games.

We were thrown together like a 'tossed salad' and began our communal living, training, and school routines. Family life made study difficult especially when three children succumbed to chicken pox at the one time! Having two boys under two years, with broken sleep patterns, didn't help either. Fatigue moved into the flat with us.

However, we were greatly supported during this time both physically, emotionally, and financially by many people. Three young girls, Katherine MacIntosh, and the Rhodes twins, Catherine and Genevieve, with their baby-sitting talents, helped us to survive and study. The St Andrews staff team, and many CMS Melbourne supporters were all so encouraging. The older two boys went with other primary school children to the nearby Princes Hill Primary School, and the younger two boys went to the creche behind the accommodation block. The training was impressive and covered a vast array of subjects and experiences designed to help us survive and flourish in another culture.

During this time, we began communicating with churches, groups and individuals to encourage prayer and financial support of us, through CMS. We had lectures on communicating with audiences and writing newsletters from Clifford Warne, the author of 'How to hold an audience without a rope.' Over his long television career spanning 40 years he produced thousands of programs for the Australian television networks. Described by a leading American producer as 'the finest storyteller', in his lectures on newsletter writing, Clifford Warne constantly emphasized the fact that 'people love stories'.

We all set about creating our individual newsletters endeavouring to use our name in the title in the quirkiest way possible. Thus *'The Touligram'* was born. It was pretty rough-and-ready in those days, produced on an old typewriter, with Letraset and draw-cut-and-paste illustrations and then photocopied. Nothing fancy like these days. These newsletters were to be sent out every three months to our allocated 'link' churches and individual supporters.

I asked a friend from Springwood Presbyterian Church, an amazingly gifted artist and cartoonist, Lyn Ferguson, if she could come up with a Touligram letterhead and a few little drawings of Wendy and I and the kids heading off to Zaïre. With a few rapid strokes of a pen, she had communicated the concepts I gave her brilliantly, in her wacky style.

One of the most enjoyable weeks, although tough, was spending a week in the Australian bush, learning how to cope in less-than-ideal living conditions. Lyn did a great job of capturing the experience in her whimsical way.

JUNGLE CAMP

Part of the St Andrews 'toughening-up' process began the second week of term when we forsook civilisation for 5 days and nights. 'Jungle Camp' - living under canvas on the banks of the Yarra, near Kangaroo Ground.

Wendy wasn't convinced it was going to be a raging success, Jeremy was just 10 weeks old. "If it starts raining I'm going to have to go home, Buddy." But it didn't. Beautiful days followed by freezzzzing nights. The boys just thought it was great. Each day we ate food from a different country - Nepali, Pakistani, Tanzanian and South American ... there really is nothing like curry for breakfast! Then there were those late afternoon baths in the river ... and everything we did was accompanied by the ever-present song of bell-birds. The daily programme included some basic classes in Electrics, Plumbing, Car maintenance, bread making,

Aspects of living on the field - eg how to make a bush toilet, purifying water, hygiene in the home, mosquito protection and injection techniques. As there were no volunteers for this last activity, we used what was available.

But for the boys the most memorable feature was killing our own chickens! We bought 14 of the scraggiest chickens you ever saw. The total cost for these feathered senior citizens was $14. It was agreed later when we came to eat them that we had been considerably overcharged.

Now, decapitating fowls is not on my list of favourite pastimes, but I thought a boil on my finger (oh groan, oh agony) would exempt me from this barbaric event. I did not reckon on the look of disappointment in my 7yr olds eyes. After all, everybody else's Dad was doing one (not to mention some of the Mums'. Not Wendy tho', she assured me that childhood memories of headless hens running around the backyard definitely put her out of the contest. So much for passing the chook!

Back to the drawing board, er, chopping block ... those eyes would not go away. Now I ask you, who wants to be a wimp in the eyes of his son. So picking up the axe and concealing my mounting disgust, I stepped forward. One last vain excuse ("I've got an infected finger on my axe-hand, so don't expect too much), fell on deaf ears. The chicken was not encouraged by that last remark. The earlier contestants in this rather one-sided match had all taken 2 or more strokes to despatch their 'opponent'. The crowd of children fell silent yet again. The axe rose. A small voice cut through the silence - "I would not ... like ... to be ... a chicken." The axe hung suspended, then fell. "Well done!" exclaimed one of the adults. There were other chickens 'done in one' that day, but for a proud 7yr they didn't matter. As the group of kids moved away, he was heard to confide to the others - "Did you see that, my Dad did it in one!" I was a little proud ... and relieved ... I too did not want to be a chicken!

The verdict on Jungle Camp ...
        hard, worthwhile, great fun!

While studying the three stages of 'Culture Shock' – the excitement or 'tourist' stage, followed by the 'frustration and withdrawal' stage, and then finally, the 'recovery' stage; we realised we had experienced all these stages, albeit mildly, at St. Andrews Hall!

We were taught that people from another culture may view us differently from how we see ourselves moving into their culture. We might perceive ourselves as having made a great sacrifice in giving up our easy lifestyle in a developed country to work in a developing country without all the comforts and 'mod cons' of 'home'. We might think we are showing love and generosity. We may think we are making an *enormous* effort to learn their language. But from their side … they may see our sacrifice as a desire to escape, or think we were unemployed in our home country. They almost certainly will see us as wealthy, even on a missionary allowance, *especially* if we have a car. They might even tell us that we are very slow in learning their language or poor in speaking it. They may tell jokes about us praying in public and running out of words and switching languages to be able to get to the 'Amen'. And it will hurt! And it did! *(We were told, only recently, by customs and immigration officials in DRCongo, formerly Zaïre, that we were only there to make money.)*

At the end of first semester at St Andrews, following numerous interviews with CMS staff, (both together as a couple and individually to ascertain whether we're 'united' in the decision or if one is not sure), on April 30, 1986, the Federal Candidates Committee, announced we had been accepted as full missionaries of CMS. Our location would be in one of the towns on the eastern side of Zaïre, the exact location would not be known until October, after consultation with the two Anglican Bishops in Eastern Zaïre, Dirokpa and Njojo.

The second semester of St Andrews Hall began with a four week 'entrée' of Linguistics taught by July Waddy, a CMS missionary from Northern Australia, and Lance Woodward from the Summer Institute of Linguistics.

Now you may remember that I said earlier, 'French was my best subject at high school'. Well, this aptitude got severely tested in this little 'phonetics and phonemics' class. We had a test. I remember it well. We had to write Nepali and Turkish words phonetically. But the way this test was marked, was severe. For *each* mistake in a *word,* you lost a mark. My final score was *Minus 19*, the worst exam result of my life! But hey, Swahili is meant to be much easier than either Nepali or Turkish. (I comforted myself with that thought and moved on to the next hurdle.)

The 'main course' for our second semester was a 'Field Survey' on the country or region where we were going with each missionary or couple presenting their final thesis or printed tome to the rest of the group.

There were also 'side dishes' along with the 'main'. Lectures on world trends in Mission, and studies on other religions. As well as that, all of us shared some of the skills we had with the others, the doctors sharing basic medical and first aid skills for those going 'where there is no doctor', technical and mechanical people sharing their knowledge on car maintenance and electrical projects, and I gave a lecture on extracting teeth, which I am sure most of them never had to use!

We all got used to having injections – Hepatitis B, Rabies, Yellow Fever, etc. Matthew was heard to confide to Michael, 'I like the ones that go just under the skin and slide along better than the ones that go straight in.'

There were moments of despair and depression, trying to study but also run a household with four active boys.

One morning I was sitting in bed, staring into my cup of tea, wondering if we would *ever* finish the Field Survey, when Michael interrupted my train of thought. He pointed to a poster on the wall.

'Daa-aaaad' he said in his singsong five-year-old voice, 'is that a photograph?'

'Yes', I replied absent-mindedly.

'We-ell, how did it get writing on it?'

I tried to explain the printing process to him.

'Oh!' A few seconds thought, then 'What do the words say?'

From my cloud of gloom, I answered …

'Keep your eyes on the far horizon, and you will find the right road!'

A few more seconds, then …

'That's kind of like McDonald's "Keep your eyes on your fries!" isn't it, Dad?'

As I struggled not to choke on my mouthful of tea, I realised my mood had suddenly changed!

'Dessert' came in the form of cross-cultural studies and experiences and we finished the course with an emotional farewell on Friday August 15th with hardly a dry eye in the place. It was a special time for us all.

THE RUBBER HITS THE ROAD

As we were about to leave Melbourne, I had an idea to improve the quality of our return trip. On the way down, it had taken twelve long, 'when are we going to get there' hours. I rigged up my video-camera (running off batteries) with the newly-acquired-for-Africa 15inch AC-DC TV (running off the cigarette lighter) and, voilà, children's on-road entertainment. Old hat now but revolutionary for us then. We had a host of the kids' favourite videos – Inspector Gadget, Mask, Short Circuit and many others and so we began the long drive back to Sydney. The three older boys were delighted, Jeremy was still too young to bother. We cut two hours off the trip. It was brilliant, the trip was a breeze. Innovation and improvisation are imperative for missionary work we were to discover.

Back in Sydney we moved into a missionary's house in Chatswood. Dr Grace Warren, known far afield and honoured for her leprosy work around the world, graciously allowed her house to be used by missionary families while she (when not away in Nepal or travelling the world) lived in the tiny flat underneath. We moved in above with four noisy boys. She didn't seem to mind.

Up to Christmas we began doing 'the missionary thing' – visiting churches and speaking at Sunday services and midweek meetings.

On these visits, we would try to answer, to the best of our knowledge, the questions of where we were going and what it was going to be like:

We will be living in a town called Butembo. It's on the Equator, at an altitude of 5500 ft (1670 m) – a pleasant climate.

There is no electricity so we are taking a small generator and a solar panel that will power some 'caravan-style' fluorescent lights in our house.

There is no town water supply so to begin, we will have to pay someone to carry water from the local water source to the house and we will store it in forty-four-gallon drums.

There is no English spoken, only Swahili and French with the local tribal language of the Nandi people who live in that region.

We will be living near two other Australian couples. Rev Brian and Ruth Fagan, who were missionaries in Tanzania for fifteen years, and now are returning to Africa – to Zaïre. Also, Brett Newell and Raya Gobius, a doctor and a nurse, arriving soon after their marriage in early 1988 to begin the Medical Service for the Anglican Church in this region.

The Anglican Church in Butembo has twenty acres on the top of a hill on the outskirts of the town. There is a large church that seats 800 people, and they are in the process of building a health centre, but at the moment it is a corrugated iron roof on pole supports, with a pile of bricks nearby.

At CMS Summer School January 1987, we spoke with enthusiasm about the work that we were going to do, *(but as yet had little idea how that work would come about)*. There was a special farewell and prayer for all missionaries that were going, including us, (even though our departure date was still unknown).

There had been plans, tentatively drawn up at St. Andrew's Hall by Federal Committee, that we would leave Australia mid-February 1987, fly to Belgium for six months French language study, before continuing on to Africa. But with a family of six, this was always going to be difficult (and expensive), so that question hung in the air for now. This February departure date would give us only six weeks for final packing and there were some serious problems with this tentative timetable.

From my point of view, there were several important factors I needed to address in preparing to go to Zaïre, and it became very obvious that six weeks was not enough time to properly sort out the details.

The first problem was the skill-set I would need.

THE RUBBER HITS THE ROAD

The type of dentistry I would encounter in Africa would require more surgical skills than I had acquired as an undergraduate and a general dental practitioner. An oral surgeon needed a three-year postgraduate course to be qualified. In Australia, any serious facial injuries, like fractures of the jaws, the patients would be taken directly to the nearest hospital for stabilization, diagnosis, and treatment by a specialist oral or maxillo-facial surgeon. A general dentist in suburban Australia would never be expected to wire a jaw. His or her surgical scope would be limited to routine extractions and some minor oral surgery. Not so in Africa.

The next two major problems I needed to face were 'what do I do about equipment?' and 'who is going to pay for it?' (Important questions.)

A dentist going to a large remote town like Butembo, 150,000 people living with no water or electricity. A country the size of Western Europe, ruled at the time by a dictator with no interest in building health infrastructure for his people. Very few dental clinics in the entire country. The capital, Kinshasa, 2000 km away to the west over a vast impenetrable jungle. No dental companies for supplies within 1000 km. And finally, no budget – this was a recipe for depression, disaster, or prayer.

I badly needed advice from someone 'on the ground' in the country where we were going. In the providence of God, there was another missionary dentist in Zaïre, and he wasn't far from where we were heading. I wrote to Martin Fugill, an Englishman, who was working at a mission hospital 300 km to our north and plied him with questions. He wrote back …

Dear Graham,

Nyankunde is a large referral hospital and nursing school. There is a four-year program to train nurses who then act as general practitioners in the local dispensaries. I have the nursing students for one week of theory and one month of practical – learning how to extract teeth. I hope to start a longer course specifically for students of dentistry. It seems to me that training is the most effective contribution that we missionaries can make to medical services here.

Village work is going to be helpful. There are many places where villagers have no dentist within walking distance, and you will be very popular with the people if you do mobile clinics.

Extraction of teeth is the overwhelming need. It constitutes 90% of treatment and people only come when their teeth are giving them a great deal of pain. The teeth are almost always abscessed and very 'broken-down'. Many of our patients have walked 20, 30, 40 or more kilometres to have their teeth taken out and they often arrive with only enough money for their extractions without allowance for antibiotics or other treatment. Root canal therapies are not feasible as we will probably only ever see them once. They will usually set off on their journey home the same day.

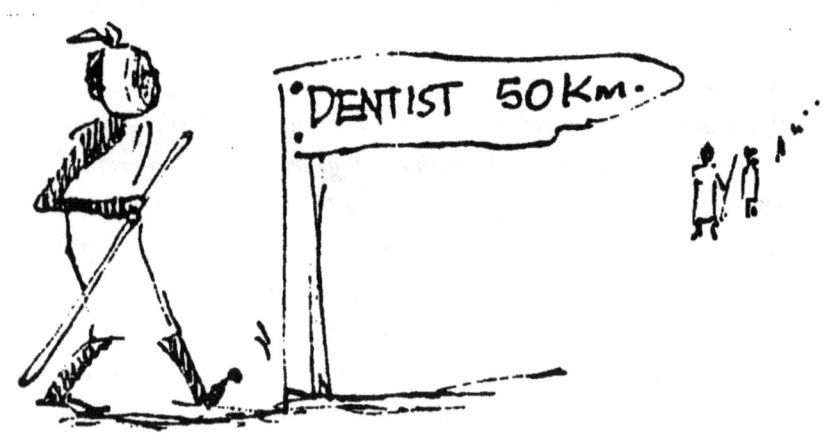

THE RUBBER HITS THE ROAD

You ask about AIDS? We have no way of testing the serological condition of people to see if they are AIDS positive. There is perhaps one case per month which is active AIDS. I take the precautions I can, gloves, masks. There is a great need for a preventive program.

Denture work is a great need – almost exclusively upper incisors. You will have to do the lab work yourself or train somebody or both.

Oral Pathology? We have a lot of infections and tumours – some incredibly large. Acute Ulcerative Gingivitis, abscesses, actinomycosis, osteomyelitis, ameloblastoma, some cases of Burkitts Lymphoma, but I have seen no oral carcinoma in the first 10 months.

Broken mandibles (lower jaws) are frequent. Maxillary fractures (upper jaws) are rare as motor cars are rare. Mandibles get broken by other people's fists. Incidentally, if you can get any training in Oral Surgery, that will make you the most highly qualified oral surgeon in this corner of Zaïre.

Supplies of equipment – there is nothing in Zaïre. Nairobi (Kenya) has a dental supply company, but the equipment is not cheap plus bear in mind the incredibly high cost of transport. Then there are customs fees and all the other ways that people have of squeezing money out of us en route.

A spittoon you can do without, a light can be made from a car spotlight run off a car battery and for sterilising we use a pressure-cooker. Instruments – bring as many hand instruments as you can! Mirrors, probes, scalers, and forceps are the important ones – especially molar forceps. A portable drill unit plus compressor and generator if you can afford it.

Also make sure you bring some good textbooks. You will have no referral service available! Any problems you face will have to be settled by you!

Best wishes as you prepare to come. I look forward to meeting you.

Martin

This was a very helpful response and gave me something to work with. It was also somewhat daunting as, in Australia, there was always help available with a difficult case. How would I go, being on my own? I'd better get as much help as I can in the time I have left, I thought.

I contacted professors at Sydney University Oral Surgery Department and the Dental Hospital, and they were most keen to help me out. I was able to sit in on 'refresher' lectures with the students and practical sessions using pigs' heads in the Oral Surgery Departments at Westmead Centre for Oral Health and the Dental Hospital. I attended lectures dealing with Maxillary and Mandibular Fractures (face and jaws) hoping that I wouldn't need them but knowing, deep down, that I probably couldn't avoid being faced with at least mandibular fractures.

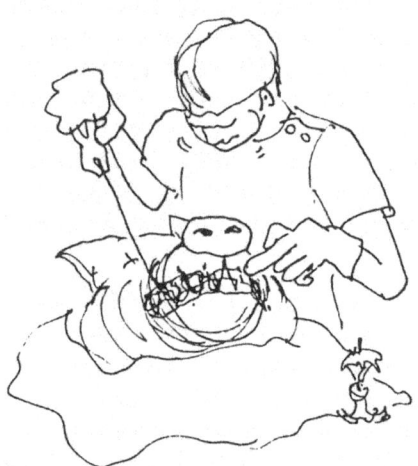

During that time, a visiting professor from Wales (a world authority) gave lectures on lumps and bumps of the face and mouth caused by conditions like tuberculosis and sarcoidosis, conditions which were common in the Bantu tribes of Africa, he said. (Now that was appropriate and timely.) This professor mentioned, in passing, that when he was training as a dental student prior to 1948 there was no cure for TB, and it was a far more infectious and deadly disease than AIDS in the 1980s. There were students each year, he added, who did not return.

THE RUBBER HITS THE ROAD

But AIDS was still a bit of a worry to a husband and father of four young children.

I got to see things in the oral surgery clinics and the operating theatre, I would not have seen otherwise. But how would I handle these things on my own? *(The feeling of being inadequate for the task was one that would not go away over the coming years with some of the dramatic and depressing cases I was to see, but for the many patients with straight-forward problems my skills, I found, were more than sufficient.)*

But the obstacle remained – how would we fund this venture? That question was yet to be answered.

SORRY ... NO AID

'Oh Graham', Geoff Lucas, the CMS Finance Secretary, approached me looking concerned. 'I'm afraid I've got some bad news. The aid we were expecting to finance your dental equipment has fallen through.'

This was March 1987.

We were *supposed* to have left Australia a month earlier for French study in Brussels en route to Africa, but due to the problems outlined earlier, CMS had decided we should stay on in Sydney for the six months French language study at Alliance Française. *(That turned out to be a crucial decision.)*

On receiving the news 'no aid', I immediately rang the dental supply company Harcourt Neil who had set up our dental surgery in Springwood in 1981. I told them what I was doing and asked if they had any portable dental equipment suitable for taking to an African village.

They had a second hand 'Adec Porta-Cart', a high speed/low speed drill unit with suction, which they agreed to sell me for $1000. A new cart cost around $12000. I told them I'd take it ... but ... I didn't have any money *yet*, but *don't sell it!*

That was a Friday.

That same night we received a phone call from Joan Twynam, a lady we had met in the country town of Taralga. She was coming to Sydney for the weekend and wanted to see us. Sunday morning she came for a cup of tea after church, and as she was leaving gave us 100 dollars.

'For dental equipment' she said.

'Oh Joan, we've been praying for funds for equipment and you're the first. I know exactly how to spend it.'

The next day coming home from Westmead Hospital Dental Centre, I called on Michael Payne. He'd had the brilliant idea of organising a 'Dental Kitchen Tea' to raise supplies and funds for us. I had begun to create a brochure and wanted to show him the rough copy. I also wanted to tell him of the generous offer from Harcourt Neil and how we had the first hundred dollars.

'I've used that type of portable unit in Papua New Guinea. They are excellent,' he said, 'You will really need something like that in Zaïre.'

With that he reached behind him for his cheque book and began to write. I couldn't see what he was writing, but I was thinking, 'terrific, another hundred dollars'. He handed me a cheque covering the remaining cost of that portable unit! I was stunned. We had reached the first hurdle and cleared it. On the Tuesday I went back to Harcourt Neil and bought the Porta-Cart.

In the weeks that followed, the provision of equipment continued. I was walking down Pitt Street in Sydney's CBD and *happened* to meet Murray McGee, an Oral Surgeon. He asked … I told him … he gave us thousands of dollars of oral surgery equipment.

Wendy's parents were keen Opera House concertgoers. They gave us their tickets for a Sunday concert 24th May 1987 – one last 'classical music treat' before we left. (They even gave us money for lunch.)

We took the train to Milson's Point and the autumn weather was perfect as we walked across the iconic Sydney Harbour Bridge towards the Opera House. Descending the steps to the Rocks area we strolled to the Opera House Concourse where, to our surprise, there was a jazz band playing. Lamb noisettes, dessert and two coffees, sun, water, sailboats and great jazz (my kind of music).

Then we went inside for Mozart, Bach for solo cello (which really is not my kind of music, but Wendy loved it), Tchaikovsky's Concerto for

Cello and Orchestra and a work by Britten which Wendy liked the most. I enjoyed it but the jazz beforehand was my preference.

But the intermission was even better. We ran into a friend from our youth fellowship days at Epping Presbyterian Church on the balcony overlooking Sydney Harbour. She was now a qualified doctor working in Public Health. As a result of that conversation, I was given a contact at the 'soon to be closed' Dental Therapists Section of Westmead Hospital. His name was Albie, and he was the Warehouse Manager. The following week Albie loaded up our Nissan Urvan with dental supplies including 4000 pairs of heavy-duty Ansell surgical gloves that were date stamped 1986. *(Those gloves, washed, sterilized and recycled, served the dental and medical work for many years.)*

The Dental Kitchen Tea was a great night at Michael and Marion Payne's home. We showed some slides and people remained conscious. Michael spoke of his experiences in Papua New Guinea teaching how to extract teeth and generally what missionary dentistry is really like. We tried to answer questions on why we were going and was our bank manager on the right track when he said we had 'rocks in our head'. There were the presents of packets of swabs and boxes of needles and the surreptitious cheques slipped into our hands at supper time.

The overall response to the brochure, the Dental Kitchen Tea and just 'word of mouth' was amazing!

8000 needles, boxes and *boxes* of anaesthetic, 40 aspirating injection syringes, more than 100 pairs of extraction forceps (40 of them brand new), mirrors, probes, and other hand instruments, Operative Kits, a large heavy-duty compressor, a 5000watt diesel generator, that *excellent* Adec Porta-Cart plus a Portable Dental Chair and light, all sorts of supplies and sundries, the 4000 pairs of gloves, *plus* $5630 in donations to buy what else was needed.

THE LAST GOODBYE

It was now July 1987 and we were packing frantically. The end was in sight, we are almost on the shorter road to Zaïre but with detours to London and Nairobi.

The 'packing anthem' went something like this …

On the twelfth day of packing my true love sent to me …
12 pairs of PJ's
11 games and puzzles
10 tubes of toothpaste
9 pads for writing
8 pencils colouring
7 Dental textbooks
6 bags for sleeping
FIVE TEN-NIS BALLS
4 school cassettes
3 trum-pets
2 violins
And thous-ands of surgical gloves!

Those final months rushed past. Life was full. Four children, two at school. Trying to keep some normality in their routine while packing up their whole lives. We packed nineteen 44-gallon drums with the necessary household and dental supplies. We crated dental equipment. We spoke every week in churches, raising interest and support. We spent precious time with family and friends. The prospect of not seeing them for three years until our first leave was daunting, especially as my father's health was failing with the scourge of Parkinson's disease and dementia.

The message that we are going for three years is sinking in. We were visiting Nana and Pa Toulmin and decided to take the van to the local car wash. Stephen, our three-year-old, wanted to come. As we were leaving, he exclaimed, 'Hooray! I'm going to the car wash. But I'll be back in three years.'

Our Farewell and Commissioning Service took place on the afternoon of Sunday 2nd of August 1987 at St Anne's Ryde. The church was packed to overflowing. In the front row of the choir pew on the right were four trumpets accompanying piano and organ and the singing lifted the roof. Significant people from our past took part in the service: Rob Forsyth, Rob Scott, Howard Whitehouse, even Michael Baughen, now the Bishop of Chester who was in Australia at the time together with his wife Myrtle. Wendy's sister Julie and three of their girls, Poppy, Anissa and Bessie, sang. The keynote speaker was the one and only Paul White, known far and wide in those days as 'the Jungle Doctor', now well into his seventies but with a twinkle in his eye and a cheeky sense of humour. He began by recalling his and his wife's commissioning service in 1938 as they were heading off to Tanzania with a young child. He said that people would promise to pray for you as you go, but what about in two months' time? So he asked himself, 'what do people do every day?' and then he urged their supporters to pray for them while putting on their shoes. He took the same concept and asked the present congregation to pray for *us* while they were brushing their teeth.

THE LAST GOODBYE

He reminded everyone that we would be working and having to think and speak in other languages and it is not easy. He said watch out for the most dangerous creature in the world, the mosquito, and he left us with verses nine and ten from Isaiah chapter 41 as an encouragement when we would be feeling 'crook' or just plain 'stonkered'. The Rev. Colin Reed did the commissioning, calling people forward to lay hands on us, a very moving finale, and then the trumpets burst forth in the final song:

> *Lord, for the years your love has kept and guided,*
> *urged and inspired us, cheered us on our way,*
> *sought us and saved us, pardoned and provided.*
> *Lord of the years, we bring our thanks today.*

We spent an incredible last week in Australia, one we vowed never to repeat. We couldn't have made it without family and friends who worked with us into the wee small hours. *(In fact, we didn't ... we were on the plane to London while they finished the task!)*

Finally, on Wednesday the 5th of August 1987, it was time to go. In a flood of tears and almost never-ending hugs with family and friends, we boarded British Airways Flight 12 to London.

We were never to see my father again.

PITSTOPS ALONG THE WAY

ALMOST ENDED BEFORE IT BEGAN

After we settled the boys into their seats, fastened their safety belts and prepared for take-off, Wendy and I reflected on the last week. That incredible last week. We had left behind twelve drums of personal belongings, seven drums of dental supplies and three large wooden crates of heavy dental equipment, with an estimated value of 40,000 Australian dollars. They were still being packed by Wendy's parents and our close friends, the Scotts.

But for now, we were on the plane and the adventure had begun. We had chosen to fly to Africa the long way via the UK for several reasons. To have a holiday before beginning this new life, to catch up with friends from our All Souls days, and to visit Lifeline Christian Mission and investigate buying a vehicle and shipping it to Butembo.

We arrived in London at 7.30am on the 7th of August and travelled with ten suitcases on the peak hour Tube from the airport. Fortunately we had help from some good friends, Mary Currie and Elrose Hunter. The older boys kept the commuters amused with a barrage of riddles and Jeremy did his best to introduce himself to everyone in the carriage.

On Tuesday 11th August I picked up the hire campervan for our UK holiday, in the back streets of London near Camden Town. I had imagined it would be in somewhat better condition. We discovered to our dismay that the vehicle had no seatbelts in the back seats and the two guys at the office, who could reasonably have been labelled 'The Dodgy Brothers', said it was the only van available and we could 'take it or leave it'. We reluctantly took the keys and sorted out the seating. The three older boys in the back unsecured, and Jeremy, now 20 months old, in the front, sharing Wendy's seatbelt.

Lifeline was located near Southampton in a village called Hedge End. We spent the morning there discussing the possibilities of buying and sending a vehicle and what type of four-wheel drive we would need.

We had lunch in the village and then headed for the motorway to New Forest. We were circling a roundabout and about to enter an approach to the M27 when screams came from the back seat.

Now any parent will know the situation. Mum and Dad have been busy all morning talking to people and the boys, particularly the younger ones, are bored stiff and getting increasingly stroppy. The parents too are getting a little edgy. Stephen, aged three, unsecured in the back, suddenly toppled off the seat as the campervan went round the roundabout. He screamed, I looked over my shoulder and was about to give him a stern command to behave and stop annoying the older boys when I felt a sharp bump. Turning back quickly, I saw to my horror that the van had mounted the low kerb and was about to plough into a metal lamppost. In that instant before impact, time seemed to stretch and thoughts ran through my mind – 'Oh, no! Brake! The boys in the back! This can't be happening – I'm a good driv…'

CRASH!

The vehicle hit the pole directly in front of Wendy. She said later she had thought that was it. The van slewed to the left and disappeared from the road, slithering backwards down a five-metre embankment. When we hit the bottom there was just the sickening sound of screaming and I was afraid of what I would see when I turned round.

'Oh God!' Wendy was crying, 'The boys!'

'You ok?' I called frantically to Wendy.

'I think so,' she said, clasping Jeremy. Together we looked back.

The inside of the campervan was completely trashed, cupboards off the walls, the back of the seat Stephen and Michael had been sitting on was snapped in two. Matthew had extricated himself from the chaos, but

ALMOST ENDED BEFORE IT BEGAN

Stephen was covered in luggage and going berserk. As we dug him out, we realised a container of salt had opened and dumped the entire contents into his mouth. Michael was lying face down on the floor and as he raised himself on his elbows, we could see his face was covered in blood. Wendy and I experienced that helpless nauseating feeling all parents have when they see their children injured.

I jumped out and tried to open the sliding door. Locked. I reached in through the front passenger door. I carried Michael up the embankment and found a vehicle had stopped at the point on the roundabout where we had disappeared over the edge.

'Can I help, I'm a nurse from the local hospital.'

She took Michael and wrapped him in a sleeping bag, and I continued to help Wendy and the other boys out of the van. The ambulance arrived and we were all taken to Southampton Hospital.

Michael's facial injuries weren't severe, but they bled a lot. He didn't flinch as the doctor gave him a local anaesthetic and stitched him up. Wendy had minor whiplash, but amazingly that was the extent of the injuries. If we had missed that pole the van would have rolled as we went over the embankment with perhaps, a more tragic result.

Matthew whispered to me while Michael was being sutured, 'Dad, this is the worst day of my life.'

The van, though wrecked inside and bent outside, was taken back to London, and returned to us 'refurbished' two days later. We attempted a very cautious day trip to Cambridge and two miles from the village of Harlow, the windscreen, stressed from the accident, imploded, showering Wendy, Jeremy, and me in glass. We limped back to London windscreen-less and the family consensus was 'we never want to see that campervan again'.

After those few weeks holiday in England, it was time to board the plane for Africa.

TOUCHDOWN NAIROBI

British Airways Flight 069 touched down on the runway at Jomo Kenyatta Airport late Saturday, 29th August 1987. We had reached Africa at last, more than two-and-a-half years since I had made that outlandish comment to Wendy ... 'we might be going to Africa.'

We had finally arrived after all that preparation. Our first day in Africa and our first impression of Kenya, after getting off the plane, was ... soldiers with guns. I heard someone shouting *'Ndiyo, ndiyo'* and wondered what they were talking about. It was only later we learnt that the word simply meant 'yes'. Our Swahili was non-existent but that was why we were in Nairobi – for fourteen weeks to study this Bantu trade language at the Swahili language school. We joined the long passport queue, finally reaching the immigration officials who were seated above us in lofty booths like high court judges. (Was this to intimidate visitors? Or perhaps that's the way the British treated them.)

It was all new to us and the kids were becoming increasingly grumpy. The next stop, with our passports stamped, was the customs desk. We had a video camera, which got through customs inspection and was allowed 'in'. But we also had a computer, given to us by friends in London, Peter and Jeanie Elliot, to help with our work. An Amstrad PC1512 – a 'powerful' computer, so they said at customs. It had 512KB of memory. *(Remember this was 1987!)* It was considered too dangerous for us to have for our three months stay in Kenya, so it was impounded, stored in a warehouse and we wouldn't see it again until the day we were leaving Kenya. This was a rather disappointing entry to the country, but what could we do?

We were picked up by CMS friends, the Rhodes family. We had trained together at St Andrew's Hall and they were now working as agricultural missionaries in Karen, the suburb of Nairobi, named after Karen Blitzen of 'Out of Africa' fame. As we left the airport, the kids were excited at spying giraffe in the adjoining Nairobi game park, alongside the main road into town.

Phil and Helen Rhodes drove us to the Church of the Province of Kenya (CPK) guest house, where we were to meet a number of other CMS colleagues who were passing through the Kenyan capital on their way home or to other parts of East Africa. The guesthouse and language school were in Bishop's Road on the hill above Uhuru (Freedom) Park behind a large concrete-block wall with an armed guard who opened the tall iron gates for visitors. This was going to be 'home' for the next 14 weeks.

Once we arrived and unpacked (a little), we started exploring the guest house and grounds. One of the first couples we met were the Milligans who, with their two boys, were on their way back to Australia for six-months leave and home service assignment following three years with CMS in Tanzania. Daryl and Jennie looked after us the first few days and gave us an informal orientation to life in Africa, and Nairobi in particular. We were keen to learn anything we could but were also aware of protecting the older boys from hearing stories and warnings that might cause them anxiety. The main warning from everyone we met concerned security.

Security in the building was pretty good, but one had to be careful walking in the streets of Nairobi, especially late in the day. We were regaled with tales of poles through windows to steal from your room, watches being snatched in the streets, cars being hijacked, and people being mugged at dusk in Uhuru Park. We had to walk through Uhuru Park to get to the CBD. Not long after we arrived, a man staying at the guesthouse walked through the park after 6pm. He entered the park one side fully dressed and exited the other side naked. The thieves stole everything!

He was badly beaten. Fortunately, the thugs were disturbed while trying to bite off his finger to take his wedding ring. Needless to say, this did not encourage us to venture into the city. But it must be said, that in our 14 weeks there we had no trouble at all. We were vigilant, keeping our bags close to our bodies, their straps wrapped around our wrists whenever we ventured outside the compound.

The first meal, we sat with a Ugandan called Abraham, who was attending an EEC (European Economic Community) agricultural conference. We started talking about AIDS, a topic of concern to a dentist about to launch into treating patients in Zaïre where AIDS had possibly originated. He downplayed its seriousness and said in his opinion 'many AIDS cases were really typhoid. Malaria,' he said, 'was a much bigger problem – AIDS is a "rich man's disease."'

We woke on the Sunday morning, to a gong being sounded up and down the corridors – all of us exhausted, sound asleep from the flight. Breakfast was 'Weetabix' and cold bacon and eggs, but we weren't complaining. Abraham told us he was going to 'church' at the nearby Anglican cathedral. So, I decided to accompany him while Wendy held the fort back at the guesthouse. She went later to the youth service at the Cathedral with Dorothy Prentice, another of our CMS colleagues working in East Africa.

One topic of conversation that kept coming up in conversations with other missionaries, was the question whether to buy a vehicle or not. Daryl Milligan and I discussed the pros and cons as we took an afternoon stroll through Uhuru Park to the city. Daryl is quite a big bloke so there were no concerns with us being mugged and robbed in broad daylight.

That night we met a Chinese surgeon who had been working in Moshe, Tanzania, and I again raised the AIDS question. He also believed AIDS was blown out of proportion so research grants and funding support wouldn't stop. However, he cautioned, he did know a gynaecologist, who was careless and contracted AIDS, and died. His advice to me was:

Wear gloves at all times.

Teach nurses to extract. You just do the 'difficult ones'.

Go slow, you will *never* complete all the work. It is better to *be there* than to rush … cut yourself … and die.

Don't allow nurses to handle anything that could cut or harm you. Handle it *yourself*.

Do the simple things and let the body heal itself.

If you have any cuts, or broken skin, *don't work!*

Be selective – there will be patients you *can't* treat. Know your limitations.

Monday morning, we met the Fagans for the first time. Brian and Ruth, formerly CMS missionaries in Tanzania, had been 'recycled' to come and work with us in Butembo. We had known about the Fagans for some time through briefings from CMS back in Australia. They came from South Australia and had arrived first in Butembo to arrange housing for us and the Newells, who were soon to be married and due to arrive in Butembo March 1988. Brian was a pastor and would work alongside the Butembo Anglican pastor, but he also had some building experience and would be overseeing the construction of our houses. Ruth was hoping to be involved with literacy classes with ladies in the parish. With their experience living in Africa and both fluent in Swahili, they were to be our mentors. We were eager to glean any information from them about life in Butembo, like where would we stay and how will we live without electricity or water on tap, along with a myriad of other questions about lifestyle and culture. There were so many things to discuss now face-to-face.

That same Monday, at breakfast, we met another memorable couple from Zaïre. People with whom we would be connected during the hard days to come. Horst and Gudrun Schultz, together with their girls, were German missionaries working with the Baptist Church in Katwa, six km from our location in Butembo.

Horst, we soon came to discover, was a German with a very dry wit. We began talking with them about one problem that was concerning us. The problem which nearly led to our demise at Hedge End – whether to buy a car or not, and if so, where. During the conversation, I mentioned we had a Nissan eight-seater van back in Australia. Would a similar two-wheel drive vehicle be suitable for the terrible Zaïre roads he was telling us about? With a wry grin, he replied in guttural English, 'You are truly a man of faith! I too am a man of faith, but I prefer four-wheel drive.'

Later during our stay at CPK Guest House we met Doug and Cathy Loden, who would become very close friends. Cathy had just given birth to their third son in Nairobi Hospital and the first time I met Doug he was sitting on the floor outside one of the toilets on the first floor of the guesthouse. His son Stephen had gone to the bathroom near their room and locked the door, but after using the toilet couldn't unlock the door to get out! He began crying out for his dad to help him. Word went through the guesthouse and people came from their rooms to help. When I appeared on the scene, Doug was talking in a very gentle and level-headed way through the door trying to keep Stephen calm, telling him it would be alright, and he'd be out soon. Everyone standing around had a solution to the problem how to get him out safely.

Someone ran to find a ladder to get up to the bathroom window from the outside. The idea was to take Stephen out the window and down the ladder to safety, but the window was quite a bit higher than the ladder and so this didn't work. Some were wondering if there would be a way to come through the roof into the bathroom. But this wasn't possible. After about 20 minutes of talking to his son, who had calmed down but was still trapped, Doug decided to 'bust the door in'. So, with all the onlookers caught up in this ongoing drama, Doug told Stephen to stand away from the door as he was going to push it open. He put his shoulder to the door and pushed. Nothing happened. He then put a bit more muscle into it and the door flew open. There was Stephen, looking very relieved.

With the rescue complete, everyone returned to their rooms with a story to tell. I got back to our room where Wendy, together with the boys, was unaware of the drama that had taken place on the other side of the guest house.

'Hey Wen, I just met this Canadian guy sitting on the floor outside the toilet with his young son locked inside. They live in Katwa next door to the Shultzes. Wait till you hear the story.'

BLOCKED GOALS EARLY FRUSTRATIONS

Four days after arriving in Nairobi, I wrote in my diary:

> 'Tuesday 1st September 1987: Feeling depressed and frustrated all day, all our energy seems expended on the boys and we are not achieving anything.'

We had sent a whole lot of unaccompanied baggage to Nairobi and we were waiting on our CMS Nairobi representative, John Hayward, a 70-something ball of energy, to help us find out where this baggage had gone. It included two bikes for Matt and Mike, and they were particularly keen to have some vestige of the past to hang on to as everything else in their lives had been removed, their young lives turned upside-down.

There was a lot of time-wasting in that first week, so we wondered what to do to keep the boys from getting bored or killing each other, or both.

'How about we go for a swim at the Hotel just across the road?' we asked the older boys. The younger ones were just happy to get out of the guesthouse compound.

It did help, sitting by that pool, even if there was an oil slick that the boys carried out of the pool on their skin and swimmers. They enjoyed the diversion and we shelled out for a six-month members' pass.

Brian Fagan was keen to pick up his own unaccompanied baggage, so we drove with him out to Wilson Airport, the small plane airport next to the game park and the headquarters for AIM-SERV, (the Africa Inland Mission Service arm), and MAF (Mission Aviation Fellowship) who would be our aerial taxi in and out of Zaïre in the coming years. While he waited to see about his luggage, I went upstairs to check on ours. Mr Solanki, who was very pessimistic about my chances of getting my luggage before Thursday, kept repeating 'big troubles', and I left feeling more depressed than when I entered.

Blocked goals seemed to be the order of the day as we approached the end of the first week in Kenya. Feelings of anger, bitterness and resentment were constantly surfacing from what was probably our first real taste of culture shock, added to the fatigue of trying to manage the emotional stability of four children ripped from their sources of security and contentment back in Australia.

'It's just the amount of tiring work the boys generate,' Wendy said to me wistfully, on her knees hand washing the nappies at 7am.

'How are we ever going to be able to study Swahili?'

Our entry into life in Africa was proving to be challenging in many ways. Each day we were meeting new people and acquiring new insights into the implications of bringing our young family to Africa.

BREAKDOWN IN THE GAME PARK

You can't come to Africa and not visit a game park … and Nairobi has a game park right on its doorstep, only 10 km from the centre of the city. So, Friday 4th September 1987, after an early breakfast, we fought with the morning peak-hour traffic (which seems to peak all day) and arrived at the Nairobi National Park at 8.30am. We paid our non-resident fees and as we drove into the African bush, a sudden movement to our left startled us.

A male impala with impressively curved horns suddenly turned, leapt across the road behind us and darted into the scrub. The trees started to thin out after half a kilometre, and we entered the flat savannah where animals from the boys' picture books began to materialise before us.

Buffalo, a large herd of 40 or more, cantered across the road in front of us.

'Look at the size of that last one!' someone yelled, pointing out an old bull with huge, curling horns.

Then an eland to the right took the boys attention, then giraffe on the adjoining hill, then warthogs with their distinctive run, tail held high like an antenna.

Herds of zebra appeared and crossed the road in front of us, eliciting the joke that every tourist to Africa cracks the first time they see them – 'Oh, look, the original zebra crossing!'

Every animal we saw, Jeremy wanted to greet.

'Hello buffaloes, hello giraffe, hello warthogs …'

We drove miles through the park, the petrol tank still showing almost half a tank as we arrived at Leopard Cliffs. As we rounded the corner, two huge buffalo appeared out of the scrub only three metres away. Putting the car in gear, we reversed gingerly so as not to spook them as we had heard buffalo can be dangerous, but this pair remained taciturn, just staring.

We continued and Matthew, consulting the *Guide to the Animals of East Africa*, identified some tiny antelope hiding in the grass along the track. 'Those are dik-dik,' he told us knowledgeably. Stephen wanted to buy one to take with us as a pet. Jeremy was just happy to greet them.

We drove down into a gully. Two giraffe sauntered down the middle of the road while over to our left was a group of baboons.

'Look! monkeys!' yelled Steve. 'Hello' responded Jeremy.

The baboons were hard at work checking each other for fleas, which greatly amused the boys, especially when they got to inspecting each other's grotesque red bottoms. We felt it was time to move on.

We had seen a lot of animals but were feeling a little cheated. We hadn't seen a lion. Someone voiced an urgent prayer that we needed to see a lion, please, God, pleeeeeeease!

Not much later we were hoping that He wasn't listening right at that time. We had been in the park over two-and-a-half hours and Jeremy was now tired of greeting all these new friends. We decided to head back to the Mombasa Road exit.

'Hey, there's a secretary bird,' said Matt, pointing out a large, long-legged bird with a ridiculous plumage of quills sticking out of the back of its head. 'Takes shorthand, types letters?' wondered Wendy.

'Hello bird,' came limply from the back seat.

My camera battery was running out, the sun was starting to beat fiercely on the car, Jeremy's 'Thomas the Tank Engine' water bottle was empty, and we turned the car towards home. We had been in some very inaccessible places that morning, but it was on the final stretch towards the Mombasa Road gate that it happened.

Cough. Splutter. The engine started to miss. And 500 metres from the gate the engine of the little blue Renault died.

'I think we have broken down,' said Michael.

BREAKDOWN IN THE GAME PARK

'Surely we're not out of petrol' I thought, the gauge is still registering a quarter tank.

I sat there. We all sat there. I blew the horn. We all blew the horn. I whistled loudly … but nobody came.

I stepped out of the car. It was at this point I remembered the boys' prayer. Suddenly I had lost the desire to see the King of the Beasts or even one of the princes. I reached reassuringly for my Swiss Army knife with its multitude of blades and selected the 'Protect yourself from a carnivore' one. I looked at it. It was only six cm long. Oh well, it would give him a nasty cut.

With Wendy steering, I pushed with all my strength and managed to push it into the next pothole. Wendy and Michael got out and while Matthew steered, with first-timers glee and a grin from ear to ear, we managed to get the car moving towards the Mombasa Road gate. When we were within 100 metres of our goal, the guards saw us and came to help.

I could not help myself. 'Er…would you mind if I videoed this?'

And they pushed us to safety.

LANGUAGE SCHOOL BLUES

The language school was in the same compound, behind the same wall, as the guesthouse. It was situated on the first floor and we were surprised that first day, sitting at our desks, to see a familiar face appear at the window. Matthew had climbed a tree and was waving to us from his position high up on one of the branches. We indicated silently but with a certain rising anxiety that he should descend immediately *but carefully!*

From the start we were deluged with grammar and vocabulary. It was like trying to drink a waterfall. Someone had told us that Swahili was an easy language, but they forgot to tell the teacher. I suppose in comparison to Japanese or Urdu, Swahili was easy, but no language is easy to master when you are exhausted from looking after four young children, in a foreign culture, and when the hard disk in your brain is full.

I had found French a much easier language because of its similarities to English and, I had learnt it at high school, over five years, at a slower pace, with a younger brain, and no two-year-old.

In our language group there were three Swedish Pentecostals, one of them a spritely 72-year-old who had been working in Zaïre for twelve years. Then there was a Marist brother who was going to Tanzania and was fluent in Cantonese after 20 years teaching in China. There was a young American couple with a small child who were going to Zaïre with the Assemblies of God and finally, a young Japanese Buddhist who was studying Swahili just for fun. I found that a little hard to believe.

There we all were in conversation groups, asking deep and meaningful questions about life and oranges and other fruit you can buy in an African marketplace. Then we would be shunted off to the Language Lab where we would don headphones and mutter strange-sounding syllables, some of which we even understood. We discovered, to our dismay, that there were eleven different ways to say 'which'. So, depending on grammar beyond my control, the word for 'which' could be 'yupi'. Or it might be 'wepi' or 'upi' or 'ipi'. Or perhaps 'lipi' or 'yapi' or kipi' or 'vipi' or 'papi' or 'kupi' or 'Donner' or 'Blitzen' or one of the other reindeer. But which 'which' is which?

'YUPI' 'WEPI' 'UPI' 'IPI' 'LIPI' 'YAPI' 'KIPI' 'VIPI' 'ZIPI' 'PAPI' 'KUPI'

Now, looking back over 30 years, I still have no idea, so I began phrasing sentences *without* clauses beginning with 'which' – much simpler.

While we were struggling with the finer points of Swahili, the two older boys, Matt and Mike, were enrolled at Rusinga School nearby and they went off each day on the bus. Steve and Jem would head off to 'Mama Nancy's School' on site each day. It had a playground which could be seen from the first-floor window in the language school. Occupational health and safety were not an issue in Kenya in 1987 and the set of swings had large, thick concrete slabs underneath the swings for children to fall on. For us, as parents, it was easier *not* to look out the window. But we did – constantly.

On one painfully memorable occasion, Jeremy, not yet two and unable to move at anything less than a full toddler's gallop, ran for the swing. He tripped over one of the thick concrete slabs and fell headlong into the swing, which cracked him in the forehead. The swing was then catapulted in the opposite direction as he continued his trajectory to the ground, striking the same forehead on the concrete block. Raising his head rapidly to begin crying, he was struck in the temple area by the swing on its return arc.

The crying began and lasted all of 30 seconds. Comforted by Mama Nancy he was off running again.

GIVE ME STRENGTH
GIVE US ALL STRENGTH

Friday 13th November 1987, with two-thirds of the language school course completed, I wrote in my diary:

    Life at the moment leaves me listless, lacking aim and enthusiasm. We try to get up at 6.30am but it's hard. Then it all begins again. Wendy or I line up for the shower while the other encourages Matt and Mike to get themselves dressed. Jeremy and Stephen sleep a little later and that's okay because it means we have a bit of breathing space to get things ready for the day ahead. Ten minutes later we drag them out of bed, struggle to get them dressed and then head to the communal dining room at 7am for the early breakfast session for those with children going to school.

    This morning, Mike doesn't like pawpaw or African porridge (uji) or toast. Matt decides he also doesn't like pawpaw and uji, but he is okay with toast. The younger ones dawdle, but we have the deadline of 7.45am for the older boys to catch the bus so we are watching the clock. As the other guests start to filter in about 7.30am, we are still struggling to get the two younger ones finished and I just want to withdraw without having to interact with a table full of strangers.

With five minutes to go before the bus arrives, we discover Mike reading an Asterix book when he should have been brushing his teeth. We then have the fight with the younger boys to brush theirs. Some days they are cooperative but today Jeremy is a 30-pound muscle fighting against me. I try to remember I am actually a dentist and supposed to be good at this type of thing. The older boys make the bus, then the younger ones are shunted off to 'Mama Nancy's School' with Jeremy screaming and Stephen dawdling behind. At this stage, which every parent has experienced, we are feeling gutted, and the day has only just begun. The last thing we want to do now is front up to a classroom to learn more about Swahili verbs, but that's what we do.

After lists of vocabulary and verb tenses, our teacher gives us our homework, which is to construct ten sentences using the 'passive' voice. Fascinating. Next, we delve into our reader called 'Binti' which leaves me totally demoralised. Wendy is looking out the window wondering how the boys are going down below in the courtyard during playtime outside. It's a bit hard to focus when you are a mum.

At 10.30am the bell rings and it's coffee time. The children have all come back inside, so we sneak past Mama Nancy's room to the dining room so that Jeremy doesn't see us and start crying again. Today I just don't want to talk to the other students or guests and feel like I am having 'withdrawal from society' symptoms. Is this sounding like culture shock or culture fatigue or whatever you like to call it?

I check the front desk for any mail. No letters again, which means no encouragement and no answers to questions from home. It just takes so long to get a letter home and get a reply. There are issues we are trying to sort out with Australia which are adding to our stress. Should we buy a car? When do we leave Kenya and fly into Zaïre and by which route? Where will we live when we finally do arrive in Butembo as the houses have not been built?

So many questions waiting for replies.

After coffee, we avoid the conversation group and both of us return to our little two-room flat to catch up on some housekeeping duties. We have been told we have to memorise 75 words and Wendy says she will miss that exam as she has too many other things to do just to keep things afloat.

I return for 'mtihani' (the exam) but the teacher, Kip, tells us a story about a crocodile and a monkey instead. Again, I don't understand more than a few words here and a few words there. My brain is trying to translate word-for-word, and it can't keep up. I get the basic meaning, I think, but I still feel like an idiot.

At lunch an African encourages me to make many mistakes with the language and says you can't expect it to happen quickly. I appreciate his kindness, but I leave the table exhausted and deflated. When you have been a professional person and you are reduced to the level of a bumbling infant in communicating, it starts to destroy your self-esteem.

During the afternoon, thank goodness, Steve and Jeremy are tired and are soon asleep. Having no energy to work on those passive-verb sentences, I try to do likewise. Wendy goes to organise a get-together for the boys with another expat mum and when she returns, the younger boys are awake, so she takes them for a visit to the back of the guesthouse where the Kenyan staff live.

Behind the guesthouse there is a compound – a large yard and a long building consisting of a number of single rooms. There is a lady Wendy has got to know who is long-overdue having her second baby. Her husband is the guesthouse driver, and they have a two-year-old child. All three live in one room and sleep in one single bed. How do they do that? I have no explanation, but it doesn't seem to worry them. She invites Wendy in for chai and spoons in lots of sugar. Wendy is good at this sort of thing but returns exhausted and a little shocked at how they live.

Meanwhile the older boys arrive home from school hungry and after a snack, start to play. Matt is brandishing a sword in a flamboyant and dangerous way in front of Mike and when he is cautioned, possibly more severely than was warranted due to stress-level-elevation, stomps off.

What's a parent to do?

Then comes the early children's dinnertime hassle at 5.30pm, followed by the bath hassle and then the bedtime hassle.

Everywhere you turn there are problems and hurdles and hassles which leave us, the parents, feeling totally impotent. I don't know if this is my midlife crisis or culture shock or just feeling a lack of support and encouragement. I don't know if the boys are experiencing their own 'junior version' of culture shock as well. I just don't know.

We reflect on when we were doing deputation before leaving Australia and everyone was saying nice things, encouraging things that kept us buoyant through the busy time of preparation and leaving, but that has all well and truly evaporated now and we are on our own. We feel frustrated being in Kenya when we want to be in Zaïre, and I am also just a little anxious about whether I can handle this dental development job that is before us.

The day finishes when all the boys are in bed and asleep and it is now time to concentrate on those passive verbs. But it is too late, we can hardly keep our eyes open. We escape to the pillow and try to get ready to do it all over again in six hours. Perhaps tomorrow will be easier.

BEWARE THE POST OFFICE TRAP

Postal slip J254915 arrived from Kenya Posts and Telecommunications, telling us there was a parcel, number DP19651, in PO Box 56292, to be picked up at the post office in the centre of Nairobi.

It was going to cost ten Kenyan shillings in duty. That's not too bad, we thought. Less than a dollar. We just have to drive into the city, find a carpark and then pick it up from the post office. That should be simple. (You can see the mistaken assumption already, can't you?) Wendy decided that as it was going to be simple, she would stay home and mind the kids after the morning Swahili class. A wise decision.

First, I needed a car.

The guesthouse had an 'amenities car' that we could hire. This was the same car that broke down in the game park, and so there was always a slight feeling of unease in the back of your mind when you drove it. However, when the options are walking through Uhuru Park, or driving a suspect vehicle, there's no contest. And doing a simple job like picking up a parcel should be a piece of cake. After all, I reasoned, we've been here a few months now and I'm getting used to this large African city and the Kenyan way of doing things.

So, I took the little blue Renault and drove down the Ngong Road to Kenyatta Avenue, the main road into town, with a certain naïve optimism. Uhuru Park, on my right, looked totally benign in the sunshine, but with gangs of unemployed youths all round, I had all the doors locked when I stopped at the main traffic lights. I found the post office building. In 1987 parking was not as rigidly policed as it is today, and so I was able to park on the footpath right outside the building.

I made my way inside, looking for the parcels' office with *the slip* in my hand. Ah, there it is. I made my way through the crowd and arrived at the door to read a hastily scribbled note saying, 'Gone to Lunch.' I enquired about lunch hour times and was told the office was due to reopen at 2pm, which was only a handful of minutes away. And besides, I had a good book, so I was happy to wait.

At *almost* the appointed time a young Kenyan girl with intricately braided hair opened the door. I showed her my *slip* and was told I was at the *wrong* parcels' office.

'So where do I go?' I asked.

'You must go to the second floor' she told me abruptly and closed the door. So I went to the second floor, up a dusty staircase as the lift wasn't working.

'I need to pick up a parcel,' I told the first person I saw.

'You are in the wrong building,' she said, and helpfully gave me instructions to get to the *right* parcels' office.

Why didn't the first girl tell me this I was thinking as I descended the dusty staircase. Suddenly a siren started wailing. I found myself in the foyer facing a police officer with a walkie-talkie directing all people out of building. I never did find out the reason for the evacuation, but I was off to the *right* parcels' office in the building around the corner.

In that building, I pressed the button for the lift, but it was taking forever to arrive so, in a state of mild frustration, I headed for its dusty stairwell. I came to the second floor and found the *right* parcels' office. A rush of relief enveloped me. Nearly there. Mission *almost* accomplished and then I can get home. I headed for the 'Parcels' sign above a large counter which we shall call Section A and handed over my *slip*.

'I'm sorry,' said another girl with even more intricately braided hair, 'but you will have to present that at the next section – Section B.'

I moved two metres to my right on the same counter and presented my *slip*.

It is here I realised I was standing next to Matthew's teacher, Miss Jackson, who was also picking up a parcel from her sister in England. We whiled away the time while someone else with intricately braided hair went to find our parcels. She eventually returned and handed over *the parcels*. (As the Kenyan T-shirt says, 'No Hurry in Africa.')

Great.

'I'll see you later,' I called to Miss Jackson and turned to go. But a man suddenly appeared from behind the counter. (*His hair* was closely cropped.)

'You will have to wait for the customs man,' he said with authority.

So, I spent more time with Miss Jackson, asking how Matthew was doing and what she paid the last time her sister sent a parcel from England.

The customs man arrived, looking important.

'Please open the package,' he ordered.

I opened the package.

The customs man picked up the jar of brown powder and asked menacingly, 'What is this?'

'It's Nature's Cuppa,' I replied. 'It's like *kahawa* (coffee). It's from Australia. My wife likes to drink it before going to bed.' (I had learnt the word for coffee just the day before so already the lessons were paying off!)

'What is its value?' he asked me.

'Ah … the label says one dollar ninety-nine Australian. That's like 24 Kenyan shillings.'

'What is this?' he said, holding up a rolled-up calendar.

'It's a calendar,' I said, stating the obvious.

'How much is this worth?'

'Oh, about a dollar. That's twelve Shillings.'

'Ah, you must pay 100 Shillings customs,' he ordered, fixing me with his gaze and looking very serious.

'I can't pay that – it's not even worth 100 Shillings. You can keep them,' I retorted.

'What is your problem?' said the customs man.

'I can't pay that. It's too much,' I replied.

He then pointed to the place on the customs slip where someone had written 'Nil to pay' in a poorly legible script and broke into a wide grin.

He knew what was going on, he was playing with me and enjoying watching me squirm.

The joke was on the *muzungu* (white man) obviously new to Africa.

We smiled at each other. He took back the parcel and gave me a second *slip* to take to the cashier and pay the duty. Not the customs, the ten Shillings duty, as written on the *first slip*.

Another girl whose hair was ... well you know already, told me that I had to take it to Counter D, which was the same counter but just around the corner to the right, and pay the ten Shilling fee for picking up a parcel. So, I took several paces to my right, around the corner, and found a surly-looking man who took my money. Retracing my steps past Miss Jackson, who was at Section C, round the corner to the left of Section A. I whispered as I went past, 'I got through the system,' and prepared to leave by the stairs.

Suddenly three clerks, from Section E at the far end of the Section D counter, came running after me and took me back to enter the *number* of my parcel in a book.

I then left by the stairs.

As I prepared to leave the building, a ground-floor clerk came running after me. She too, (with intricately braided hair), needed to *register* the fact that I had indeed picked up, paid for and was about to depart with parcel DP19651.

(We greatly valued that Nature's Cuppa, which lasted some weeks, but the calendar lasted us for a whole year.)

I got off easy. But not so poor Miss Jackson. Her sister (what was she thinking?) had sent her shampoo, conditioner, and some vitamin pills – total cost about ten or fifteen Australian dollars. The postage cost had been 30 dollars and the customs duty was 114 shillings, *another* ten dollars! I arrived home and Wendy asked, 'How did it go?'

'Oh, no problem ... well, actually ...'

THE WEDDING MIX-UP

We were invited to a wedding on Friday 11th December 1987. This was a 'big deal', as the bride was the daughter of Mr and Mrs Kivuti. Mrs Kivuti managed the CPK Guest House and Language School where we were studying and Mr Kivuti worked in the office of the President of Kenya, the Honourable Daniel Arap Moi. Not only that, but their daughter Emily was a graduate of the Nairobi Dental School and her fiancé a member of the Kenyan national soccer team. This was a high-profile wedding.

You may be wondering why two low-profile students from the Language School were invited to this rather prestigious event in Nairobi life. You may be excused for assuming it was for our scintillating conversational contributions in Swahili, newly learned, like, 'Bring me food Bwana,' or 'How much is that orange?' or 'Hey taximan, take me to the supermarket.'

It could have been ... but it wasn't. It was my video camera. Mrs Kivuti saw me one day using my Canon, now old and clunky, but then very modern and extremely chic with an imposingly bulky camera attached by an umbilical cord to a large VCR recorder slung over my shoulder and hanging at my waist. (I looked very professional.)

'Would you mind,' she asked politely, 'coming to my house (that is it over there next to the guesthouse), next Friday? My daughter Emily is getting married. It would be very kind if you could help us in this way.

My daughter was to have been married last Saturday, but Kenya made the final of the All-Africa Cup (very exciting news), and her fiancé was needed to be playing against Tunisia. They played very well. And won too. So you see, the day *had* to be changed.'

Of course, I agreed, and after purchasing a new videotape for the outrageous price of 30 dollars (320 Shillings), I dutifully turned up on the morning of the wedding. I circulated with the camera among the waiting guests while Wendy sipped *marakuja* (passionfruit) juice and made small talk about oranges and taxis and going to Zaïre to work. We were free for the afternoon as the older boys were still at school and the two younger ones were at Miss Nancy's Nursery School. We were greatly enjoying this cross-cultural experience. An hour passed. Nothing was happening. There is only so much you can ask about oranges.

All of a sudden two minibuses arrived from near Mt Kenya, full of people from the Kikuyu tribe, (the main tribe of that area). The Kivutis are Kikuyu, and it seemed like things were about to 'get going'. I positioned myself with the sun at my back, while the women all assembled by the gates of the CPK Guest House and started singing an African song of welcome, swaying in time. From the gates they approached the house and for the next 45 minutes danced in front of the bride's house. The bride, I was told, was 'pretending' to hide and didn't appear during this time. Someone arrived with crates of sodas – Fanta, Sprite and Coca-Cola – and handed them out to all the guests, including Wendy and the cameraman. Everyone sat on the grass under the trees (out of the hot sun), waiting for the groom to arrive with his entourage. Sipping sodas, waiting for something to happen.

The groom, it needs to be explained, was from the Luo tribe. The Luo, we are told, will arrive to *claim* the bride. But it is Kikuyu custom to refuse (at first), to release the bride so everyone can see how much she is valued by her family. There would be a mock battle, a kind of genteel scuffle, when the groom and his groomsmen would try to wrest away the bride. A truce is declared, and the groom's family proceed to placate the bride's family by laying 'kangas' (brightly printed African fabric) on the ground. The bride then walks over these kangas so she doesn't 'dirty her shoes' on her

THE WEDDING MIX-UP

way to the car. The bridal cars then take them all to the cathedral at the bottom of the hill on the edge of Uhuru Park for the wedding ceremony.

All that was meant to happen at about 12.45pm, with the arrival of the bride at the church timed for exactly 1pm.

But the problem was ... *that* marriage ritual is a *Kikuyu* custom, but *not* a Luo one. The *Luo* custom is for *their* family to wait at the church for the bride to be brought to the church by *her* family. A clash of cultures which strangely, it seemed, hadn't been foreseen or discussed.

So we waited, and waited, 1pm came and went, and we waited until sometime after 2pm. Frantic phone calls were being made behind the scenes. Then finally, the groom's family 'gave in' and arrived at the Kivuti house with much singing and waving and that incredible African rhythmic movement of bodies that Westerners can only yearn for. There was the scuffle, then the kangas going on the ground and the bride was able to leave the house and enter the wedding car. Everyone heaved a sigh of relief as we proceeded to the church.

(It did seem a little incongruous that after all this wonderful African chanting and singing, upon entering the church the organ boomed out and we all sang, in a somewhat unemotional way, 'All people that on earth do dwell'!)

Then, with the video camera whirring, the Kikuyu dentist and the Luo soccer player were duly and properly wed.

KWAHERI KENYA

It was 7am, our last day in Nairobi, 17th December 1987. We were packed ready to fly to Zaïre, having completed the 14-week language course. Phil Rhodes had organised to get us all to Wilson Airport by 7.30am for the MAF flight to Bukavu.

MAF were one of the few airlines flying into Zaïre, and they were to become our regular connection with the outside world, bringing mail and occasional supplies and eventually providing an escape route during times of turmoil. *(But that was years away and we were blissfully unaware of what was to come.)*

We had become good friends with Phil, his wife Helen and their three kids, now in their early teens, during the cross-cultural training we did together in Melbourne, and we had enjoyed these three months near them in Nairobi. We had some fun times in their twin cab, visiting the Nairobi National Park on several occasions, especially one jaunt chasing a rhino down a gully and cross-country to get *the photograph*.

That same Datsun twin cab entered the CPK carpark and came to a stop in front of our pile of bags. A short, red-bearded man with a huge smile climbed out of the cab.

'Good morning travellers,' said Phil, jovial as always.

'Beautiful day to fly to Bukavu,' he said as he opened the tailgate on the canopy, pushing the back window up and extending the bracket for support. He moved a 22-gallon drum of fuel, placing it on the tailgate, making it easier to get the bags in, and then began loading our luggage.

'Careful with that large vinyl bag, it's a portable dental chair,' I said.

'It's in good hands with me' said Phil, giving me a wink.

SMASH!

Shards of glass went in all directions.

The bracket arm had collapsed, and the rear window came crashing down on the fuel drum. Datsuns of this vintage do not have safety glass, and tiny jagged fragments covered Phil's head. They were in his hair, in his ears, down the back of his shirt. Fortunately, he had turned round and there were none in his eyes.

Then we started laughing.

We brushed him down. No cuts. By the time we had everything sorted it was well after 8am.

'Don't worry,' said Phil, 'John Hayward is already there, and he will make sure MAF don't leave without you. Anyway, this is just another TIA experience.'

TIA?

'This is Africa ... expect the unexpected.'

We all laughed again. Then the six of us squeezed into the *four* passenger seats and off we went.

'I guess you now get to see whether the Swahili lessons paid off,' said Phil as he pulled out through the CPK gates, smiling cheekily.

Groan, I thought. Phil knew exactly how we felt about our time at language school, as necessary as it was. (But him being a Kiwi and we being Aussies was always enough reason for a bit of good-natured teasing.)

'Who said it was one of the world's easiest languages, that's what I want to know,' I replied.

'But the word is that *Zaïrian* Swahili is easier than Tanzanian or Kenyan Swahili,' said Phil.

'I hope so' I replied, 'anyway, I should be able to get by with French.'

'We'll be right, Buddy!' encouraged Wendy who, on reflection, had spent a lot more time at language school being a mum than being a student, more time changing nappies than parsing sentences!

It had not been easy for any of us.

KWAHERI KENYA

The CPK Guest House provided basic accommodation for our large family but Nairobi often had water shortages and power outages. There had been a violent riot outside the locked gates of the compound one particularly day. Then there were the difficulties of learning a new language, often with untrained teachers. Not much homework was done after school hours – by the time the kids were fed and in bed, exhaustion took over. My final score in the Swahili exam of 62% was acceptable, but I was not about to set the world on fire as a linguist and Wendy got a 'mother's exemption'.

One of the ongoing frustrations that quietly concerned us during our stay in Nairobi was learning from the Fagans that Brian, in his early sixties, trying to organise the building of two houses, was having to walk the three or four kilometres into town every time he needed any building supplies. After sourcing the supplies, he would need to organise a truck to pick them all up, and then walk back home. We desperately needed a vehicle, any sort of vehicle, for the three families to survive.

But for now, language school was over, we were flying out and we were happy to say *kwaheri* (goodbye) to Kenya and *bonjour* to Bukavu, Butembo and life in Zaïre.

Wilson Airport is the 'light plane airport' in Nairobi, situated on one side of the National Park, outside the Kenyan capital. It is about 30 km from the main international airport, named after the first President of Kenya, Jomo Kenyatta.

Wilson is very small in comparison to Jomo Kenyatta International Airport, and with all our luggage, including the portable dental chair and two boys' bikes; it didn't seem unreasonable to drive up to the entrance and offload all the bags in front of the customs building rather than parking a hundred metres away and 'man handling' it in (there being no trolleys). In fact, the day before, we had unloaded several other bags in the very spot where we were now parking, having asked one of the airport staff who had smilingly agreed. So, we returned to that same spot close to the entrance.

'You can't park there!'

A cantankerous airport official came running towards us.

'But I asked yesterday and was given permission to park here and drop off some bags.'

'No, it is not permitted! You will be in very bad trouble.'

'Where is the person in charge? Could I speak to them please?' I asked politely. He left, disgruntled, to seek his superior.

While he was gone, we unloaded our large amount of baggage and proceeded to stack it in front of the Customs and Immigration office. The cantankerous official never came back. Did we win that round of 'the game'? Maybe we did. Others of the airport staff were friendly and welcoming, some of them very interested in our 'safari' to Zaïre.

Once inside the gate, we looked round for the person who would help us through the formalities, John Hayward. He was already inside and soon appeared, his long scraggly white hair surrounding a large balding area on top. He came rushing to meet us with the unbalanced gait of someone needing a hip replacement.

'Sorry we're a bit late,' said Phil, 'we had a bit of problem with the back window that isn't there anymore.'

John Hayward was the go-to man for CMS. A missionary, well past retirement age, but despite his age, still bubbled with the energy of someone 25 years his junior. He was the one who met you at the airport, who knew where to buy a water filter or a bucket shower or a portable autoclave/pressure cooker; he was the one who did the myriad odd jobs to enable CMS missionaries arriving from Australia to prepare for their onward journeys to upcountry Kenya, or Tanzania, or Uganda and now the new team heading into Zaïre. He was invaluable.

'No problem, but we'd better get you weighed in quick. The sooner you get off the better. The weather is fine now, but the clouds come in quick and it's a four-hour flight.'

'I thought it was only three hours to Bukavu.'

'You are stopping at Mwanza on the way, Barbara Spring is on the flight.' Barbara was a delightful older CMS missionary who had been working in Tanzania for 35 years.

'Lovely,' said Wendy. 'We haven't seen her for ages.'

'How are you boys feeling today?' John asked, directing his smile at the older boys. The two younger boys, Steve and Jem, had gone to investigate a garbage bin.

'Excited ... Great,' chorused Matt and Mike.

As we pulled the nine bags out, John noted 'You've got a lot of stuff. Hope you are not over the limit.'

'I think we have about three hundred kilos.'

A flicker of anxiety crossed my mind.

Inside the MAF office, the friendly office worker placed each bag on the scale, noting it in the log. 'What is this?' he asked, pointing at a large, awkward, grey vinyl bag with reinforced edges.

'It's a portable dental chair. I'm a dentist going to set up a clinic in Zai-i-ray.' (I used the African pronunciation.)

'You have a lot of baggage. This adds up to 430 kilos.' He paused and broke into a smile.

'But today you are blessed. The plane is not full.'

Next stop Customs and Immigration. This is where the fun begins, I thought, casting my mind back to the day in August when we had first arrived in Nairobi and they confiscated our computer. We assumed they thought it was a security threat, these newfangled machines with luminous green writing on a black background. Or maybe they just wanted a bribe. We didn't know. We were new to this game. We didn't offer a bribe. We didn't get our computer.

The previous day, after fourteen weeks, we had gone through the hassle of getting the computer from Jomo Kenyatta Airport so that we could leave the country with it. We were learning that processes are almost always convoluted and difficult to organise in this continent. (But we were here, and we just had to learn.) Mr Odero, who seemed to be in charge, could not have been more helpful.

We left the pile of luggage, including the two bikes, outside and entered the customs office. A stern-looking official took my handful of passports and began to study them. He paused and looked up at me, his lips pursed, and his brow furrowed. His fingers drummed the desk. 'You have a problem!'

'The game' had begun again. With sweat breaking out on my forehead, I explained to the customs man what we had been doing in Kenya. I explained what we were going to be doing in Zaïre. I used some of the Swahili I had been taught. I hoped it might help, but my Swahili wasn't that good. I explained about the computer, and the dental chair, and where we were going. Eventually, with MAF officials entering the office to remind the customs officer the flight must take off before the weather worsened, the officer relented, stamped our passports, and pushed them across the table. The transaction *he* had hoped for, had not taken place, and he was not happy.

As I opened the door to leave, a junior office worker pushed up against me and whispered in Swahili, 'Utanipa zawadi ya Noeli' (You will give me a present for Christmas). I wasn't sure whether this was a question or a command. I gave him a blank look, shrugged my shoulders and pretended I didn't understand. I stepped outside. The customs official followed me.

The MAF Beechcraft had arrived and parked nearby.

The official looked at the bikes.

'Where is your permit for those bikes?'

'We don't have a permit.'

'You can't take those bikes out of Kenya without a permit,' he insisted. This got us *rather* upset.

'We brought them into Kenya through a company called Notco,' I explained.

'Yes, the company handled our unaccompanied baggage three months ago!' Wendy added.

'We obeyed the rules, Notco has the details, and Mr Odero out at Jomo Kenyatta said there was no problem. So what is the problem now?'

When we mentioned Mr Odero's name there was a momentary pause, and we thought we were through 'the game'. But no!

Coming at the situation from another angle, having been unsuccessful from his previous attempts at extracting some monetary gain from the situation, our 'friendly' customs man demanded, 'Where is your inventory for these things?'

Well he obviously didn't know about Wendy's administrative skills. She had anticipated such a request and stayed up very late the night before typing up on the guesthouse's old typewriter, a list of all our belongings. He pursed his lips and furrowed his brow.

'Where is the copy for our office?'

Inward groan. He is kidding, isn't he. No, he's not.

'We only have the one copy,' I offered.

'You cannot leave on your flight unless you have a copy of this list for our records,' the customs man replied tersely.

'Can we use your photocopier?' Wendy asked.

'We do not have a photocopier.'

Naturally, we both thought. Why would an office have a photocopier? No surprise. We turned away and walked back to John and Phil.

'Can one of you take me back to the MAF office to get a photocopy? Fair dinkum, this is frustrating!' I muttered.

We sped the kilometre to the MAF hangar, got the copy and returned to the plane, everyone including the pilot waiting patiently in the shade. No money changed hands and as we emerged from the office, longing to be on the plane and 'out of there', we noted the pilot had carefully loaded all the luggage on board the Beechcraft, securing it with straps and a net.

We said our farewells and, though sad to be leaving some of the few friends we had in Africa, we eagerly clambered on board. Buckling up the younger boys' seatbelts, before strapping ourselves in, while Matt and Mike looked after themselves. Then the MAF pilot spoke over the PA.

'Welcome aboard the flight to Mwanza and Bukavu. We'll have a short prayer and be on our way.'

NO STOPPING NOW

BONJOUR ZAÏRE

The MAF Beechcraft taxied to the runway, was cleared for take-off, accelerated, lifted off and banked over the Nairobi National Park. We had spent many happy weekend hours visiting the Park with our six-month pass during our stay in Nairobi. A last look at the herds of game – antelope, zebra, giraffe and buffalo scattered across the large expanse of African savannah on the outskirts of Kenya's national capital. They were quickly becoming black dots and disappearing in the distance as the twin-prop plane climbed to an altitude of 12000 ft.

We passed alongside the Ngong Hills of *Out of Africa* fame – the four hills that the local inhabitants in years past took to be the knuckles of a giant's fist rising out of the earth. We flew into the magnificent Rift Valley, heading towards Mwanza, the first stop on our way to Zaïre. From this vantage point, the pilot announced, if the weather conditions are right, you can see Mt Kenya in one direction and Mt Kilimanjaro in the other. Special, but not today. Too much cloud.

We landed in Mwanza, a large town in Tanzania on the shores of the vast Lake Victoria. There we dropped off Barbara Spring and Carole Evans, two fellow CMS Australia missionaries. Then we were in the air again. The excitement levels of the boys (and the parents too, just quietly) was rising as we approached beautiful Lake Kivu and the city of Bukavu.

Whereas tones of brown predominated in our glimpse of Tanzania, the countryside we were approaching was multiple shades of green covering the beautiful hills and mountainous country of eastern Zaïre.

Jeremy, dressed only in a disposable nappy (diaper), was reaching his limit on this three-hour flight and lapsed into a reasonably good-natured little sing-song chant … 'Geddout, Muuuummy! Geddout Daaaaaddy! Geddout Muuuummy!'

Matt and Mike were fixated on the countryside as we were landing, pointing out the strange and the familiar.

'Look at all those banana trees! Man, there are bananas everywhere.'
'I love bananas.'
'Hey, there are gum trees like in Australia.'
'Can we build a cubby house Dad when we get to Butembo?'
'Look at that old rusty tin shed over there. I wonder what it is?'
'Who are all those people in front of the shed Mum?'
'Hey Dad, there are soldiers everywhere – with guns.'
'Can we have lunch soon? I'm starving.'

As we taxied up to the tin shed which turned out to be the Customs and Immigration office, we could see Margaret Lawry, our Zaïre team leader, a seasoned CMS missionary who had worked in Tanzania in previous years. With her was David Boyd, from Melbourne, a theological lecturer and keen Hawthorn fan; and Geoff Stanbury, an electrician who we knew from his work on the technical team with Neil Brain at NSW CMS Summer Schools.

Our first impressions as we climbed down from the plane and scanned the surroundings were: some familiar smiling CMS faces mixed with some unsmiling officials; a large crowd of children craning to see the new arrivals from behind the airport's barbed-wire fence; alongside some serious, threatening faces on soldiers brandishing AK47s, lounging against the buildings nearby. All around, hills and greenery, mud huts and thatch roofs, aged Belgian buildings decaying and crumbling. Electricity wires dangling from poles, going nowhere. It looked to us like a war zone – without tanks and artillery. No new buildings. No fresh paint. Dust and dirt everywhere. Everything looked run-down, rusty, ramshackle.

'Gidday!' 'How's it going guys?' came the broad Aussie male greetings.

'Welcome to Bukavu Toulmins,' said Margaret, smiling broadly and trying to look encouraging, as if she knew something that we didn't but soon would. The boys gave 'Auntie Margaret', whom they had got to know back in Australia, warm hugs. We all shook hands, glad to finally be in the country that we had been talking about for the best part of three years and meeting up with the first group of the Aussie Z-team members.

'Are you ready to face customs? It should be fun with all that stuff!' came the amused comment from one of the guys looking at the 430 kilos of luggage being unloaded from the Beechcraft.

A SHORT HISTORY SINCE COLONIAL TIMES :~
(A COUNTRY WITH MANY NAMES)

1885 BERLIN CONFERENCE ~ KING LEOPOLD II ➤ "**CONGO FREE STATE**" EXPLOITATION
1908 WORLD OUTCRY OVER ATROCITIES - BELGIAN GOV'T TAKES OVER ➤ "**BELGIAN CONGO**"
1960 **INDEPENDENCE** President KASUVUBU P.M. LUMUMBA ➤ "**REPUBLIC** OF **CONGO**"
1961 LUMUMBA ASSASSINATED **1965** JOSEPH DESIRÉ MOBUTU ~ COUP D'ETAT
1971 AUTHENTICATION ~ NAMECHANGES: MOBUTU SESE SEKO ➤ "**ZAÏRE**"
1997 FIRST CONGO WAR ~ KABILA SNR OUSTS MOBUTU ➤ **DEMOCRATIC**
       SECOND CONGO WAR ~ 1998➤2003 5 MILLION DEAD   **REPUBLIC** OF THE
2001 KABILA SNR ASSASSINATED KABILA JNR ➤ PRESIDENT
2006 FIRST ELECTIONS - JOSEPH KABILA **2018** TSHISEKEDI   **CONGO** (DRC)

ARTICLE FIFTEEN

The rule, we had been led to believe, was that all personal effects should be free of customs duty. That didn't mean they *would*, just that we had been led to believe they *should*.

In our naivety, (even though we had done our survey of Zaïre at St Andrew's Hall), we were not really familiar with the workings of 'Article 15'.

At this point of the story, I need to help you understand a little of the long, complicated, and overwhelmingly tragic road the people of this large African nation have walked since the days they were first colonised.

In 1885, at a conference held in Berlin, European powers divided Africa, deciding who would 'take' what countries and where the borders would lie, often following geographical markers like rivers and mountains, with complete disregard to tribal boundaries. There were *no* Africans present to represent their interests.

Amongst the decision-makers was the Belgian king, Leopold II, who had ambitious plans to stake a claim, not for his country but for himself. With guile and subterfuge, he convinced the other country representatives that he would, as a 'humanitarian venture', take the central African territory known as the 'Congo'. It became known as 'Congo Free State' and was the second largest country in the continent, bordered by nine other countries. Over the next 23 years he exploited the people for the rubber and ivory so viciously, so inhumanely that millions perished and there was a worldwide outcry against the atrocities committed.

In 1908, the Belgian government took control away from Leopold and it became known as the 'Belgian Congo' for the next 52 years. But their rule was harsh and bureaucratic with little feeling for the people and no interest in training them.

With independence movements happening all round the world, Congolese agitators were called to Brussels in February 1960. The Belgian government picked an arbitrary date, June 30th, to give the country back to the Congolese people – giving them just four months to prepare. (There were only 16 Congolese university graduates in the entire country at the time.)

Independence Day came and Prime Minister Lumumba seized the opportunity, with the Belgian king present, to decry the previous decades of Belgian rule, castigating them for their cruel subjugation of the Congolese people. It was one of the great but most undiplomatic speeches of the twentieth century. Within six months Lumumba was assassinated.

Within five years Joseph Mobutu staged a coup overthrowing the government and his increasingly kleptocratic rule destroyed the country over the next 32 years. He failed to provide any paid public services like health, education, police, and military forces (except the soldiers who kept him in power). There was no maintenance, so the road system set up by the Belgians and maintained by the local communities fell into disrepair, and travel became more and more difficult. Communication within the country was poor to non-existent, meaning it was easier for Mobutu to maintain control. Despite vast stores of mineral wealth, the country plummeted to become one of the poorest in the world.

'Article 15' is the well-known but *unwritten* article of the 14-article constitution of the 'Mobutu era'. In French, *'Debrouillez-vous'* and translating into English as, 'Look after yourselves'.

In 1971 Mobutu decreed an 'Authentication' movement throwing off the vestiges of western rule to become more authentically African. He changed the name of the country, the major river, and the currency unit, to 'Zaïre'. The capital, formerly Leopoldville, became Kinshasa. Western names and western dress were outlawed.

ARTICLE FIFTEEN

'Article 15' was basically 'carte blanche' for anyone in a position of power to extort money from people under their jurisdiction who required a service of *any* kind. Even just travelling on a road or being in the wrong place at the wrong time, you could end up having to pay. It was extortion *of* the people dressed up as service *to* the people. Everyone, and that includes the soldiers with guns, had to provide their own income. Human nature being what it is, together with the 'modelled' history, meant it was not always done in an equitable manner! We were about to meet 'Article 15' face-to-face, but we were totally unaware of it at the time.

Putting on our best smiles and greeting the customs men in Swahili, *Jambo* (hello) and *Habari gani* (what's news), we presented our 'goods' for inspection. There were two customs men, both unsmiling, both grim, brothers in intimidation. 'The Brothers Grim'. (There would be no 'fairy-tale' ending, we suspected.) The boss, dressed in a scruffy uniform, and his henchman began work on our 430 kilograms of luggage.

The first promising sign that we might *just* have 'a fairy-tale finish' was when they overlooked the boxes holding the new computer we had been given by our friends in London. This sinister instrument of espionage with its ability to destabilise a government, as I have said earlier, was an Amstrad PC1512 with 512KB of memory on large floppy discs and a dot matrix printer. Surely these Zairian customs men are going to want to look in *those* boxes. But no, just at that time, Geoff and David began to talk most earnestly in Swahili with the 'Grim Brothers' about the state of the nation, the economy and whether they had seen the latest *Star Wars* movie. It worked. They pushed the boxes through and turned their attention to a suitcase, the contents of which were strewn all over a rickety desk.

'We knew it,' said one of 'The Brothers'.

'This cassette player is a very valuable electronic device. You must pay at least 100 American dollars duty,' said the other.

This is when the 'David and Geoff routine' came into play again. They explained that the *bwana* here has had this cassette player for more than two years back in Australia and seriously, it is an old cassette player of the type that nobody would pay duty on and the fact that it is nice and clean is because Australia doesn't have dirt roads. All the roads there are covered in bitumen like in the town of Bukavu (but without the holes), so you can see that it is old but clean and therefore doesn't require the payment of any duty. *Asante sana* (thanks very much).

This little 'conversation' (or confrontation) took over an hour, but like all good or bad things, it did come to an end, and the 'Grim Brothers' were somewhat grimmer when we left.

We loaded our belongings and the dental equipment into one vehicle and our family squeezed into David's car for the drive into Bukavu. 35 km of bitumen road, hills and bends and banana groves. Greenery everywhere. Avocado green, moss green, fern green, forest green, jungle green. Green, green, green. It was wet season and the mountains of South Kivu sparkled in the aftermath of an afternoon shower. The wet season in Bukavu, unlike some of the more arid parts of Africa, lasts for eight or nine months of the year and there is constant cloud and fog around the mountains that surround Lake Kivu and Kahuzi-Biega National Park, the home of the mountain gorilla, 30 km to the west. As we were driving, I wondered if I would get to see the gorillas during our eleven-day stay in Bukavu.

It would be a shame to be so close and miss out!

Bukavu is a beautiful city, or it was when the Belgians 'ruled' and built more than a hundred Art Deco buildings. Now looking rather drab, with paint peeling, the glass windows grimy from wood fires and dust. The position of the town on the south-western shores of Lake Kivu however is spectacular – especially from 5000 ft when you are flying in. It looks an idyllic place to live and work.

We entered the main street of Bukavu like yachts competing in the America's Cup, tacking back and forth to avoid the cavernous potholes that pockmarked the once-bitumen surface, and which made travelling at more than 10 km an hour impossible. Cars travelling towards us were also zigging and zagging and it was just a matter of missing the potholes and the oncoming cars; but at the limited speeds there was little danger.

'There are lots of shops,' we observed.

'Yes,' responded David, 'but they only have limited goods at any one time. A *commerçant* (businessman) will travel to Dubai and return with certain 'lines' like toilet paper, Nescafé, shower caps, paint, glue, and that is what is sold in his shop until he makes another trip. There are very limited supplies of 'luxury goods', but I have heard it is much worse in Butembo. At least here we are close to the Rwandan border and many more things are available over in Cyangugu.'

We continued driving, asking more and more questions. Suddenly David was aware I had my video camera out the side window.

'Don't take any photos or video,' warned David, but it was too late! I was filming the 'road' and the other drivers in the 'yacht race' with my Panasonic 7.

'Pull over,' said the policeman who had seen me brandishing my 'weapon'.

'You are in big trouble,' he said in French, which translated meant, 'Now is your opportunity to provide for me and my family for the next several days.'

And that was when David went into his spiel. 'These are the new missionaries from Australia who have been invited here by Bishop Dirokpa. You know Bishop Dirokpa, the Anglican bishop?'

'Bishop Dirokpa!' cried the policeman, 'why, he is my brother.'

So we all got out of the car and greeted the policeman and agreed that it was a great thing he was the Bishop's 'brother' (which probably means 'distant cousin') and therefore one of our best friends and we were out of trouble. No 'Article 15' here. We acknowledged his position of power and recognised the wonderful job he was doing with some fluent smiling and bowing and scraping. Then, relieved, we climbed back in the car and proceeded up the hill towards the Anglican compound and the Bishop's house to greet and be greeted.

GORILLAS IN THE MIST ALMOST MISSED

It was decided – we'd do it!
But not all of us.
David, Keren (David's sister visiting from Australia), Margaret, and I left early for the 30 km journey to Kahuzi-Biega National Park, an hour on the Zairian roads from Bukavu. After paying the park fees we were assigned an English-speaking guide called John and joined a group of six others, most of whom were European.

'Where do you come from?' John asked the four of us.

'Australia,' we proudly replied.

'But you can't be Australian,' he exclaimed, 'You're … clean!'

He was used to having low-budget Australian tourists visiting who were doing the safari treks on the back of trucks over several months with limited opportunities to wash.

We started, the mountain looming ahead. Upwards. Slowly. Entering the forest, the only paths were the ones made by the gorillas. Through thick jungle, climbing over moss-covered rocks and dodging vines, like the jungle I remembered from Tarzan movies of my youth. At the start it was rather exciting, but it wasn't long before it was just plain hard slog. The jungle had closed in around us and progress was slow.

There was very little to encourage us we were on the right track for the silverback male and his harem except the occasional nest where he had slept a few nights previously. Always a few nights before. Where was last night's bed? Finding the gorillas' dung was a breakthrough and we marvelled at the size of it – like a loaf of bread. Then suddenly, after three exhausting hours, there was a rustling in the bushes ahead of us.

Stop, signalled John, his finger pressed to his lips telling us to be silent.

We moved forward tentatively and after some minutes caught a glimpse of the back of an adult female. Then she was gone through the undergrowth.

That was it. A brief back-view encounter with a diminutive female. We could hear grunting in the distance and John confirmed *that* was probably the silverback. Push on.

Entering a leafy clearing we came across several females and their infants. John once again signalled to us to move softly and slowly and we made our way through the clearing. The noise of breaking branches – and there he was. The silverback. The lone dominant male. We had been warned that if we did encounter the gorilla and he wanted to display his dominance, he could mock-charge us.

'If he charges you,' said John, 'don't move. Hold your ground. It's just a bluff.'

Right, let's get that straight. Don't move. Hold your ground. With a 270-kilogram gorilla charging. Right!

We were now in the clearing, faced with this huge primate. And he was irritated. We moved slowly forward. The gorilla was only metres away. John signalled us to stop. The silverback was hunched over and began picking up handfuls of leaves and tossing them, at us, the intruders to his domain. And then it happened.

It took only a fraction of a second. He lunged in a gesture of aggression, then charged. We all dived for cover.

Stand your ground. I don't think so John!

Don't move. I don't think so John, when all his teeth are 'bared', and he's coming at you at speed.

Fight or flight? Flight took over.

The silverback's rush was only momentary, a feinting charge to scare us, and then he turned away and lumbered slowly up the track, back to his family.

I started the camera rolling and panned round the group. They were all ashen faced, except for John, who was laughing fit to burst. When the camera settled on Margaret, she squeezed out, 'Well that was a bit scary, wasn't it?'

We returned to the car in silence.

Mike, watching the video later that day, commented during the final scene as the huge gorilla waddled up the track, 'Gee Dad, he would need a big toilet seat, wouldn't he!'

BUTEMBO AT LAST

The time in Bukavu was a fun-filled and significant time for us all. Jeremy had turned two the day after we arrived and was fussed over by an extended family of adults and children, both Australian and Zairian, our first birthday party in Africa.

The Christmas Eve service at the Anglican cathedral which began at 11pm and finished at 1.10am Christmas Day was something of an ordeal for parents and children alike. Christmas Day was another long service, but the Christmas presents Wendy had bought before we left Australia made up for it. After two services in Swahili, the boys knew the Gloria, 'Utukufu kwa Mungu,' off by heart, their hands swinging back and forth like a metronome. *(They could probably to this day sing parts of the chorus.)*

We had for some months been trying to wean Steve off his night-time dummy. Rational argument had failed, but it happened at the Boyd's house in Bukavu – but not in the way we thought. Succumbing to pressure from his older brothers, Steve threw his dummy into the Boyd's chicken coop – for the chickens to use. A nice gesture we thought!

Michael lost his first tooth that Boxing Day in 1987 while we were visiting the Anglican cathedral situated in the suburb called 'Essence' – he was investigating the crypt at the time!

For ten days David and Prue Boyd's house was abuzz with the sound of children's games played with squeals of delight and the occasional brouhaha, which is only to be expected with kids. The cooking was especially appreciated after 14 weeks of guesthouse food and our boys ate them out of house and home. We loved the big Bukavu bananas, buying a stick of 147 for less than three American dollars, which was polished off in three days. It was a lovely time of fellowship, fun, frivolity, and fruit.

The morning of Monday the 28th December 1987 dawned clear, sunlight reflecting off the perfect surface of Lake Kivu. Today was the day we would see Butembo for the first time. We had of course seen several slides taken by Peter Dawson when he visited some years before and knew a little of what to expect; but today it was really happening. There was sadness mixed with excitement as we farewelled Margaret and Keren, Prue and Narelle and the kids.

David and Geoff drove us to the airport only to find our MAF flight was delayed by an hour and a half. We sat in the shade of the hangar, feeding the boys while stopping them from killing themselves climbing on everything in sight. Eventually the blip in the northern sky became a shape and then the small six-seater Cessna landed and taxied to the hangar.

'Hi, I'm Joe Hart. The Toulmins, isn't it? Pleased to meet you. Sorry for the delay. Had to get a patient to hospital. Now ... how much of this stuff can we get in the pod and how much in the back of the plane? We're coming back on Wednesday, so the bulkier things can come then. Now for the six of you. We'll have to double up with two to a seat in the middle. Wendy, is it? Right. Wendy if you can hold the youngest – how old is he? Ah, Jeremy is just two, okay! Last week? Happy birthday Jeremy. Wendy, you and Jeremy in that seat, the two older boys can share the other seat and Dad can hold this blondie here. What's your name? Oh, Stevie. Well Stevie, you can sit up front with me and Dad and help me fly this plane to Butembo.' Stevie beamed. 'Daddy and Deevie,' he chirped.

Joe loaded the plane with practiced precision and then squeezed us all into our allotted seats. 'You can put on those headphones and we can talk on the way,' Joe offered. I was trying to juggle Steve plus the video camera on my lap ... getting the headphones on was a little awkward.

Joe activated his radio and called his wife who was back at the base in Nyankunde, 'flight-following'. 'One plus six for Butembo,' he said, and then guided the plane out to the runway and took off.

'That's Butembo ahead,' said Joe, pointing to a large town centred in a valley between many hills in the mountainous region of North Kivu. 'The population is over a hundred thousand – it might even be a hundred and fifty. The main tribe is the Nandi. They're an industrious tribe, many businesspeople among them.'

We were flying over houses which looked picturesque from the sky but very different on the ground. Most were mud and thatch, but some here and there had corrugated-iron roofs, some rusted, some shining brilliantly in the sun. The houses often had surrounding hedges and studded the hills along the main dirt road which passed north to south through the commercial and market area of the town and headed the 55 km north to Beni, the next major centre.

We started to descend, each of us peering intently out the windows looking for the Anglican Church, the landmark we knew from the slides. Then Joe banked the plane sharply to the left and a grass strip appeared in front of us with patches of red gravel, and with a bump we were down and taxiing towards a large open hangar at the far end of the strip.

We could make out Brian and Ruth Fagan, our senior missionaries who'd arrived three months earlier. Standing alongside them was a young Zairian pastor and next to him were Doug and Cathy Loden, the Canadian Baptist missionaries we had met in Nairobi at the CPK Guest House. The government official came towards the plane as the propeller slowed to a halt but, unlike the customs men in Bukavu, this time there were no problems thanks to that young Zairian pastor!

'Welcome to Butembo,' smiled Ruth Fagan.

'This is Pastor Ise-somo,' said Brian, and we shook hands with the man who was to become our best friend and mentor over the next few years.

We greeted Doug and Cathy warmly while our kids and theirs got reacquainted and went off to explore the large hangar and the sheds nearby. More crowds of children had appeared with the arrival of the plane. They were straining to get closer but were kept at a distance by an airport official with a large stick.

As the bags were being removed from the pod under the plane, a land rover came thundering up the dirt track and screeched to a halt. Out jumped an enthusiastic young Englishman called Gordon Cutting, who had come to Butembo to manage the local office of the coffee firm ESCO, which also sold chickens, eggs, and cheese brought in from Goma. We were to become very friendly with Gordon along with Philip and Deborah Betts, the other expat staff of ESCO who were stationed in Goma, 300 km to the south. Gordon had come to help transport the mountain of luggage that had accompanied us.

Joe Hart farewelled us all with hugs and handshakes, wished us well, climbed back into the plane, and taxied the tiny Cessna out onto the runway. With a roar of the engine, he accelerated down the red gravel strip and rose into the air, the plane seeming to drop first at the end of the runway before rising and climbing and eventually disappearing from view.

As I watched the plane go, I looked around at Wendy and the boys heading for the vehicles to take us to our new home and I remember thinking, 'I hope this was a good idea.'

THE BIG WELCOME

We were fascinated by the sights and sounds as we drove the four kilometres to the Anglican 'hill', dominated by the instantly recognisable church in front of a large grassy area used by the kids for football games.

After almost three years we had finally arrived.

The procession of three cars turned right into the large Anglican property on top of the hill at Kitulu, a suburb of Butembo, a city built on hills. The cars continued towards the church where a large crowd was waiting, pulling up in front of a brick building – the almost completed nurses' quarters. This was to be our home for the next eight months while Brian Fagan supervised the building of two new houses, located on the other side of the church.

As we started to get out of the cars, the crowd surrounded us and began singing songs of welcome. Hordes of children, all fighting for the best view of the 'white newcomers' and their children. The ladies continued singing, one seeming to direct the choir. Her size and personality made her stand out. Mama Leah was her name, we would learn, and she was certainly larger than life. A big personality to match her size.

There was handshaking happening everywhere and our boys were looking on in astonishment. They too were mobbed with lots of the local children trying to touch a hand or arm or face.

More children came running from everywhere and soon there was a crowd of 400 kids all crying out *'Wazungu! wazungu!'* (White people! white people!). *(We are still met with this greeting by Congolese children even to this day!)*

We were led into the church by Pastor Ise-somo for a service of welcome. Ise-somo began with a speech saying how much they appreciated us coming to help with a dental clinic in the health centre, and then Wendy and I were both expected to greet those gathered in Swahili. At this stage the young pastor had limited English and we had limited Swahili (with a bit more French), so we managed with a mixture of the three languages. Then more singing and dancing, with us needing little encouragement to join the happy throng.

At the conclusion, the church leaders were introduced to us one by one – Mzee Kyuma, the chief elder (his name and title were pronounced M-zay Chooma – Mzee being a Swahili title of age and respect), Sampson (whom we had met in Nairobi months before – he was the only English speaker among the group), Sampson's brother Japheth and finally Enosh, all smiling and pumping our hands.

We moved outside and the throng of kids moved into our personal space again. It started to become a bit overwhelming for Jeremy and Steve in particular. The touching and the pinching disturbing them. Pastor Ise-somo quickly took control, directing the crowd to keep back and leading us to the nurses' quarters. Steve and Jem squeezed through the door first and the older boys followed, looking around at the whitewashed walls and the sparse furnishings. The four boys were then off exploring every room and deciding where they wanted to sleep. The adventure had begun for them.

While the kids did the tour of the inside, 400 faces were competing for space at the windows, running from window to window, chattering and laughing as the boys entered the different rooms. Willing hands from the Lodens and Gordon brought in all our luggage, with Wendy and I keeping a close eye on the crowd of kids, so things didn't 'go missing'. Once everything was safely inside, we too 'toured' our new home.

THE BIG WELCOME

There was that 'gulp' moment when we surveyed the emptiness of the building. Both Wendy and I extrapolating what would need to be done to transform it into a home.

The building had cement floors and glass in the windows, which for a local house was impressive, but those were all the 'mod cons' it contained. No curtains, no furnishings, no kitchen, no bathroom, no toilet could be found in the nurses' quarters.

The nurses' quarters had been built with a recent TEAR fund grant. A 'fired' mudbrick building constructed using cement rather than mud mortar with a shiny new tin roof. On the right of the building was the front door, which opened into a largish entrance room, the 'salon', with two smaller rooms opening into it. The one on the right had a back door leading outside. On the left-hand side of the 'salon' there was a central corridor with two rooms on each side. The salon had a table and six chairs. It was basically a shell and if it hadn't been for the Baptist missionary families and Gordon Cutting lending us what furniture they could spare, we would have had nothing except the six stretchers that were part of our luggage, along with two small *jikos* (cooking stoves), two buckets bought in Bukavu, a Tilley lamp like we used to have when we went camping as kids, two Aladdin-type kerosene lamps and a bucket shower.

We were led down the corridor to see the four rooms that would be our bathroom and bedrooms. There was nothing in any of the rooms. Wendy and I again thinking the same things but nodding encouragingly to the pastor and church leaders. 'Muzuri, muzuri' (good, good) we said, while thinking 'strike a light'!

The kids were running in and out, shouting, 'This is great. It's just like camping.' We are smiling wanly and saying, 'Yes, it's just like camping.'

'And Mum, Dad, we can build a cubby house outside really easy.'

'That's terrific boys.'

The tour of the main house complete, we were led outside through the back door to see the kitchen building, which was smaller and about five metres away. It had three rooms – the first room was full of ladies with some charcoal *jikos* making chai and what looked like an evening meal. They looked up as we entered, greeting us warmly.

On one side, on the concrete floor, there was a metre-square brick wall about 30 cms high which they explained was support for a 'cooking plate' – a piece of flattened 44-gallon drum we could easily acquire from the main market in town, only three kilometres away. 'Wendy Toulmin, this is your kitchen!' went through my mind.

The next 'outside' room was a storeroom (empty) and the third room, also empty, was for the *'zamu'* or night watchman who would be arranged for us by Pastor Ise-somo.

Then, still in a state of semi-shock mixed with total amusement we were led around this building and down a grassy slope to the toilet.

Ise-somo, we realised very quickly, was a delightful man. He smiled, raised his hands in a gesture of 'sorry, but…' and apologising profusely in Swahili and broken English, explained that the long-drop toilet wasn't quite finished. We looked at the half-built brick construction with a ten-metre 'long-drop' inside, over which the builders were putting a suspended concrete floor with a hole in the middle. We replied in English and broken Swahili that it would be fine, we would manage somehow. He continued, saying he hoped we had some other way of looking after those needs, or that is what I think he said, but I wasn't quite sure; and he explained, I think, that if we were desperate there was another 'long-drop' at the Archdeacon's house just a hundred metres away. 'I'm sure we will manage,' I tried to say to the pastor – all the while thinking about that sturdy red bucket with the lid we had just brought from Bukavu.

Back into the house for a welcome cup of tea, which Isesomo told us the ladies were preparing out the back in 'Mama Wendy's new kitchen'.

The house was by this time full of people all wanting a piece of the action with the arrival of the new dentist's family with all those boys. All the windows were still crammed with kids peering in. There was much smiling and handshaking. We were *very* thankful when the pastor announced that we were very tired from the travelling and people should leave us now to *pumzika* (rest).

The locals gradually dispersed, and we were left with just the *wazungu*, (the 'white people') of the Australian, Canadian, and English tribes. Over that cup of afternoon tea, we thanked Gordon and Doug and Cathy for all their help with the vehicles, the transporting of our luggage along

THE BIG WELCOME

with the loan of the furniture we were sitting on! They too then left us in the house with just our kids and the Fagans.

But the ladies remained in the kitchen out the back. Late in the day, they provided a huge meal for us. Chicken, fish, rice and vegetables all in separate pots cooked on the charcoal *jikos* in Wendy's outside kitchen.

We shared that first meal in Butembo with Brian and Ruth. It was the first of many. The Fagans, we discovered, had four adult children, similar in age to ourselves. They were grandparents too, so our children were to become proxy grandchildren over the years to come. They had spent many years with CMS in Tanzania and their Swahili language skills were excellent. We would have been lost without them especially in the months that followed.

FIRST BED-TIME

After the meal, the Fagans returned to their house behind the church and we set about getting the boys ready for bed, as parents do. However, this new environment required some thinking and planning about how to do 'the bedtime routine'.

There was no electricity, so we were reliant on those two kerosene lamps and the Tilley lamp. The boys quickly worked out their bedrooms – bigger boys in one, younger boys next door. The bathroom was chosen, the first room on the left down the corridor. Mum and Dad got the other room off the corridor. Right. That's done. Now for the bath. Jeremy had a baby's bath with a teddy bear sticker on the side. We placed that in the corner of the bathroom. We rigged up the bucket shower Geoff Stanbury had made for us while in Bukavu so we could stand in the baby bath and use the limited amount of water … Wait a minute, we haven't got any water, except for the boiled water in the two Thermoses. The boys will have to go to bed dirty. Not really our biggest problem at the moment, we reflected.

'Okay you can all go to bed without a bath tonight. Now … everyone must go to the toilet.'

'But Dad, we don't have a toilet, what do we do?'

'It's simple. See that sturdy red bucket in the corner of the *bathroom*? Let's pretend that's the toilet.'

'It's okay for ones, but what about twos?'

'That's why I called the bucket *sturdy* – you can sit on this bucket.'

'But you can't sit on a bucket Dad. What if it tips over?'

'Yes, that *is* a design fault and is probably why buckets never caught on as toilets. But it'll have to do. You just have to be careful.'

'Dad, he's not peeing in the bucket. It's going up the wall.'

'Hey, be careful where you aim. Don't pee on the wall.
Who's going to clean that up, eh? That's better aiming, well done you.'

'How do you sit on this thing Dad?'

'You just have to squat and balance.'

'I can't do that Dad. This is no good. Why can't we have a toilet like back home that you can sit on and read books?'

'Just do your best and – oops, are you okay? Man, that was lucky. I nearly had to clean up a big mess, didn't I.'

With the boys' *help* we set up the stretchers and, using the chairs from the Lodens as a framework, draped the mosquito nets over them. We all crawled into our sleeping sheets on our stretchers under our mosquito nets and instantly fell asleep. It had been a big day.

I didn't sleep well that first night.

I kept dreaming that one of the boys got up in the night and kicked the bucket.

EARLY DAYS

In the morning all was well – my dreams had not been realised. The kids were still asleep when I clambered awkwardly out of the stretcher and mosquito net 'tent'. Wendy was already up, adjusting the wicks on the small kerosene 'jiko' to boil water from the Thermos for a cup of Nescafé instant coffee – the jar we had bought in Bukavu. (We need to ration each spoonful till we ascertain if Nescafé is available in Butembo.)

I wandered round the empty shell that was our temporary home and couldn't help shaking my head.

'Oh my goodness Wen, they didn't tell us this on the tourist brochure.'

We both laughed. We'll be right. Little by little.

Little by little, the boys surfaced from sleep and Wendy set about preparing what food we had for our first breakfast in Butembo. We would have to get used to not having a fridge – leftovers don't last. Once fed, the boys were off outside to explore again, followed everywhere by the ever-growing crowd of kids, the two older boys striding out confidently in front, the two younger ones trying to keep up.

As we cleared away the remains of breakfast, Wendy said 'I'll go into town today. Ruth told me she and Brian are going and I need to check out the market and get some things. The ladies who were cooking last night said they'd be back today. They left some 'bidons' (yellow plastic jerry cans) of water and will keep them filled for the next few days, but after that we're on our own.'

'How are you getting to town?' I asked. (The issue of a vehicle still very much on my mind.)

'Brian said that Mzee Kyuma will lend him the old green ute that we used yesterday to bring our luggage from the air strip' she replied.

Matthew came running in, followed by Mike, Steve and Jem bringing up the rear with bare feet, having jettisoned his shoes. We *had* told the boys about 'jiggers', the tiny dust mites that burrow into feet and then produce an itchy sack of eggs that has to be removed with a safety pin, but for a two-year-old the words had little impact.

'Mr Chooma just arrived in his ute'.

'And he's got a goat in the back' Michael added excitedly.

'Yes, it's really big' added Steve.

'Yes, it's as big as me … and, and it's got a black spot on its head.' (Jem wasn't going to be left out.)

The crowd of kids following parted as Mzee Kyuma arrived at the door and called 'Hodi' (the equivalent of ringing a doorbell or knocking loudly). In his hand was a rope tied round the neck of a large black and white-spotted male goat.

'Karibu, Karibu, Karibu Wageni' (Welcome newcomers) he beamed. *'Hapa ni zawadi kwa jamaa yenu'* (Here is a present for your family) and he handed me the rope.

'Asante sana' (thank you very much) Wendy and I chorused with one of the earliest Swahili phrases we had learnt in Nairobi. A lot of African-swivel handshaking and head-touching-head followed (a sign of friendship). The boys are very excited. We have never had a goat before. (I thought I wouldn't share with them the fact that the *'zawadi'* was to be the main course at a coming feast.) They all vied for the privilege of holding the rope, dragging this very large goat away from the front door to find some grass. The entourage of kids of all ages followed in a chaotic mass.

We invited Mzee inside and I grabbed one of the Baptist missionaries' chairs and invited him to be seated, smiling all the while. Taking another chair, I sat down for my first experience of hospitality on my own. Wendy had disappeared out to the back kitchen to find the two thermoses filled with water she'd boiled on the 'jiko' at breakfast along with the little sugar and milk powder and that precious jar of Nescafé. Meanwhile I tried to make conversation in my limited Swahili with the most important man in the church and one of the main identities in the town. A bit daunting to say the least!

Mzee (everyone, Brian had explained the day before, just calls him Mzee) only spoke Swahili and his tribal language Kinandi, he had no French so already I was at a disadvantage. There was lots of smiling and awkward silences as the two of us struggled to find words to connect. I thought I understood what he was saying, something about the car and the market, but I keep tripping over the vocabulary in my mind. I kept smiling and nodding although I really didn't understand the exact message that he was trying to get across.

Just as Wendy was laying out the cups (also loaned to us by the Baptist missionaries) and pouring hot water from the thermos on top of those precious brown granules, Brian Fagan poked his head around the door, followed by Ruth. They both greeted Mzee with all the appropriate greetings in their fluent Swahili. I was saved and happily allowed them to shake hands and begin chatting as Wendy searched for another two cups. Ruth, after greeting Mzee, went out the back to help Wendy with the 'hospitality', meagre as it was at this early stage.

After *chai* and chat, Wendy and Ruth, squashed into the ute, Brian climbed into the back and with Mzee at the wheel, they headed off to town while I tried to find the boys with the goat.

The days start early here. At the first sign of light, people are on the dirt road outside our house going to and fro, especially on market days, Wednesdays and Saturdays. Men pushing bicycles laden with fresh fish from Lake Edward, a long steep walk down the mountain to the lake 80 km away. Women coming from distant villages laden with bananas, cassava, leeks, tomatoes, and other vegetables balanced in basins precariously on their heads. Young girls heading to the water sources with their 20-litre yellow 'bidons' (pronounced 'beedons') also balanced on their heads. There is a well nearby, about 500 metres away, but only for 'washing water', we have been told. The main 'clean water' source is two kilometres away, on the road to the airport. (We would still need to boil and drip filter this 'clean water' for drinking.)

Young boys in blue shorts and grubby white shirts kick rolled-up banana-leaf soccer balls in impromptu games on the field across the road before school. School starts early in the morning for half the school with the other half coming in the afternoon. The school assembly happens about 100 metres from our home. The uniformed students lining up and singing President Mobutu's praises with the raising of the Zairian flag, accompanied by the singing of the National Anthem in French. *(This was to become a regular part of our lives every morning at 7.30am.)* Posters of the President's face are everywhere, in tiny shops, on walls, fences, in every home, every office, every school room.

Doug Loden and his two older boys arrive for a visit in his white Landcruiser provided by the Canadian Baptist mission. Having come from Australia where just about everyone has a vehicle and where we are used to going where we want when we want, the whole issue of mobility was a predominant worrying thought in my mind (and had been for some time remembering the UK detour on the way here). How do we get around? How do we get things done? Do we have to rely on borrowing Mzee's car? How do we get to the market especially thinking of the number of things we need to find and buy to get our household even somewhat functional? It was hard to look at Doug's vehicle without a touch of envy. But we are missionaries, I remind myself, you don't think that way. A touch of envy? I push the thought away and greet Doug heartily.

He speaks English to me, it's like music to my ears. Being in a total Swahili environment is really tiring even after only one day. It's wonderful to hear a language that I understand every word.

Wednesday is the day the MAF plane comes in (if the weather is good). It's the day to send mail back to Australia to assure the parents, the

CMS bosses, and close friends that we have made it safely and that we are 'settling in', although we don't report how much 'settling in' is required.

'How are you folks surviving?' Doug asks with a grin in his Canadian drawl, as his boys ran off to find ours.

'Not bad' I laugh, 'but we have a long way to go before we have a functional home. It will be good when the extra bags and the bikes arrive today – Matt and Mike have been wondering when they'll get their bikes. Not to mention the dental equipment, it will be so good to have that portable chair here in one piece after such a long journey via London and Nairobi. But there is just so much basic 'stuff' we need – *if* it's available.'

'The plane is due in about 30 minutes. Is it okay with you and Wendy if I just take you and leave my boys here to play? There won't be room for your luggage and the bikes if I take all the kids.'

On returning from the airstrip, the boys were very excited to have the bikes and were off riding around the football field in front of the church, the younger boys running behind with the Loden boys.

Doug and Wendy headed into town. The second shopping expedition produced four single and one double foam mattress along with some buckets, basins, and those yellow plastic bidons for carrying water. (Pastor told us he is organising for a young girl to come and do that 'daily chore' for us.)

It seems strange, but we are slowly getting used to calling people by their job description – I get 'dentiste' (said with a French accent) and Wendy gets 'Mama Matthew', which I guess to the locals is *her* job description. We don't call Pastor by his *post nom* Ise-somo or by his birth-order name, Muhindo, which is the 'Nandi' name for a boy born after a girl. (Mobutu, we were to learn much later, in his 1971 'authentication' directives, outlawed 'Christian' names which the earliest missionaries had instituted.)

New Year's Eve, Pastor calls in early in the morning and tells us it's necessary we go into town and present ourselves to the Commissaire, the head man in town. Greeting people is very important in African culture, he tells us, *and* it is very important to fulfil the formalities demanded by the Government for 'outsiders' coming to stay in Zaïre.

Mzee arrived with his ute (Pastor only has an old bicycle) and off we all went, fighting with the potholes of the dirt roads leading into town. We come to a 'main' intersection and turn right onto the road that takes you to Beni, 55 km to the north and Goma, 300 km to the south.

The main street of Butembo looks like it came straight out of a Wild West movie set except there was no Clint Eastwood. The shops, which extended along the main street for about two kilometres, were dilapidated, rundown, the buildings being a throwback to the time the Belgians ruled the country. The ute pulls up in front of an important-looking building with a Zairian flag out the front, the background bright green with a forearm holding a burning torch. Alongside is a once-impressive sign announcing the Commissaire's office in French, now covered in dust.

I follow Pastor into the Commissaire's office where he introduces us and there is much handshaking, heads touching, joking, and laughing. The language used here is French and I feel a little more comfortable as I greet the most important man in town and bring greetings from my wife who is home with the children and from our family and friends back in Australia, especially our CMS mission leaders. He seemed to understand my French with the obvious Australian twang. He is very welcoming and assures us that the people of the town are looking forward to having a dentist.

'There is much suffering among our people' he adds, 'not only from toothache but from the untrained village practitioners who often do more harm than good'.

Formalities completed, we shake hands and leave the building.

The next stop is the Immigration Office where we begin the process of getting a 'Visa D'Etablissement' – a process, we have been told, that will be long (up to a year), and expensive. 'This is where Article 15 surfaces again,' Pastor explains, 'as the staff in the office are not paid – like the schoolteachers, the police and so on.' He smiles and shrugs his shoulders.

We head home and Mzee tells Brian we can use the vehicle in the afternoon. His chauffeur will drop it back to us around 2pm.

Wendy had lunch ready and as we sat round the table, I asked an obvious question.

'Do you want to go to the market this afternoon boys?'

'Yay!' came the enthusiastic response.

The ute was delivered as promised and Wendy and the younger boys squeezed in the cabin with Brian driving and the older boys and I sat in the back. There are no rules here about seatbelts or carrying passengers on the tops of trucks or the backs of utes. The older boys loved it.

We are all taking in the new sights and hearing the strange sounds. Goats nonchalantly meander down the street looking for scraps of food. Sheep, oblivious to the dangers, wander aimlessly on the road in amongst the traffic. There are only a few cars, but lots of 'beat-up' trucks with dust clouds in their wake. Advertising signs painted on many of the buildings look 'tired', the windows covered in dust, like in Bukavu. One thing I notice straight away – there are lots of pharmacies dotted along the street – selling drugs is obviously big business here. There are boys struggling to push strange wooden barrows and large 'scooters', with wooden wheels, over-loaded with goods. Women with every conceivable article balanced on their heads. People going in all directions. Men shouting and gesticulating, arguing and cajoling. Pursuing their different business plans, buying and selling, finding spare parts, looking for a deal that would bring them some Zaïres, the local currency (regularly devaluing); or even better, American dollars. Other men lounging in the shade playing chequers on makeshift boards (with bottle tops for the playing pieces) or drinking 'pombe' (banana beer). A soldier, with his semi-automatic rifle slung carelessly over his shoulder, shouts and directs the haphazard traffic at the town's 'round point'. Fascinating activity everywhere. A colourful chaotic mêlée. Our eyes were consuming everything.

Wendy had said 'wait till you see the market' and it certainly exceeded our expectations both in size and the availability of fruits and vegetables. The boys went off exploring with great enthusiasm, returning with stories of goats being butchered. Their heads sitting on the dirty counters of little 'dukas' (wooden sheds), covered in flies. And everywhere, bright orange palm oil is being sold – heated in open-topped barrels to stop it solidifying.

We came home exhausted. Using another language all the time and having so many new and unusual experiences is tiring and makes you want to withdraw to your 'safe place'. The boys were starting to 'unravel at the edges' by the time we pulled up in front of the nurses' quarters.

That night Gordon came for dinner and then he and I, assisted by the older boys, rigged up the mosquito nets *properly* – a real hit with all the boys, who are now 'sleeping in their caves'. Apart from that it was a very quiet New Year's Eve.

New Year's Day 1988, Pastor again arrives early. This time to inform us we need to go to church today 'to welcome in and give thanks for the New Year'. (The service went for two-and-a-half hours and we hardly understood a word!) The sermon went for almost an hour, but just watching Pastor was enough – what a speaker! He's certainly able to hold an audience without that proverbial rope Clifford Warne told us about! We were welcomed and I again made a short speech in Swahili which Wendy had written while in Nairobi.

We didn't seem to achieve much in those early days. Just getting the kids fed and doing basic jobs seems to take all day as there is a constant stream of visitors.

So it was a big day when our 'helpers' arrived.

The household started to stir around 5.50 am when Matthew began trying to get me out of bed. 'It's too early Matt' did not stop the urging. Steve and Jem had already woken hours before and had deposited themselves in our 'bed' and began playing 'Let's see who can kick Mum and Dad the hardest'. Fortunately, we were too tired to rouse ourselves and after a short grumble, 'why can't they stay in their own beds', fell asleep again to dream of flushing toilets, light switches and a vehicle to go shopping in.

I eventually gave up trying to sleep and dragged myself out of bed to make a cup of instant coffee using the Thermos. Then, after the normal waking routine which involved that red bucket again, I had a shower standing in the baby's bath using some of the precious 'thermos water'.

EARLY DAYS

While I'm in the shower and water is spraying to all corners of the room designated 'bathroom' (but which has no drainage), there is a knock at the door and someone is calling out 'hodi, hodi' (are you home?) and 'jambo' (hello) repeatedly.

It was a young girl who introduced herself to Wendy as 'Unnie' (Annie). *(I will meet her later.)* She had been told by Pastor Ise-somo to come and carry water for us. It will be her task to fill our two 44-gallon Teflon-coated drums from the well 500 metres down the hill, which we will use for washing water. She carries two bright-yellow plastic 20-litre containers, bidons, at a time and does 10 trips.

Apparently, Annie was not due to come till 7.30, but if you don't have a watch and the sun is up, you turn up. She almost caught us napping.

Then at 7.15am a man turns up, catching us mid-porridge. Smiling ingratiatingly, he introduces himself as 'Ferdinand'. If he had been able to understand English this is what he would have heard … Stephen (who now doesn't eat porridge) yells 'Can someone cut my toast?' at the top of his voice. Michael (at the same time) groans 'My head hurts.' Jeremy (having spilt porridge all over himself) pleads 'Gedda washa.' Meanwhile, Matthew is doing his 'meal dance', where his rear end never actually manages to touch the chair as he balances first on one foot on the rung of the chair, then on his knees then does a handstand on his elbows, up, down, wriggle, wriggle until the end of breakfast.

After the last mouthfuls of porridge, the boys have gone out to play and it's time for Wendy and me to start training our new 'helpers'.

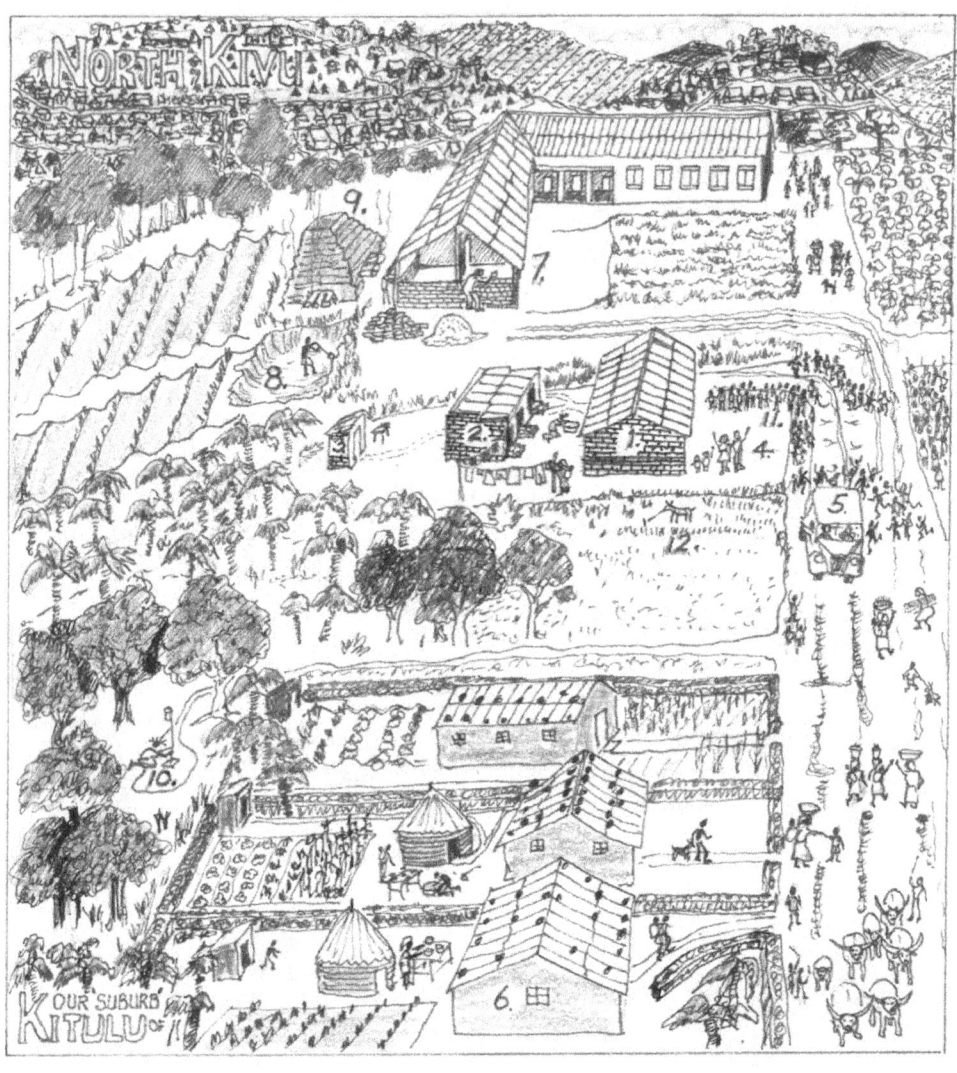

1. Our home for the next 8 months in the future nurses' quarters. 2. Wendy's outside kitchen, the storeroom and nightwatchman's room. 3. The unfinished 'long drop' toilet. 4. Jeremy and Steve, Wendy and me. 5. Doug and Cathy Loden and their boys visiting. 6. The Archdeacon's house – he is away studying in England. His wife, Faith, has been very welcoming. 7. The Anglican Health Centre where the dental clinic will be located – it was completed in August 1988. 8. The pit where they dig the mud to make the bricks for the health centre building. 9. Burning the bricks in the brick 'pyramid'. 10. The well where Annie gets the washing water. 11. There are always children watching us. 12. The goat we were given as a welcome gift by Mzee Kyuma.

13. A large grove of eucalyptus trees. 14. The city of Butembo in the distance – 3-4 kms walk. 15. Ladies walking to and from the market carrying baskets, and bowls on their heads filled with vegetables, often with a baby strapped to their backs. 16. Brian and Ruth Fagan 17. The Anglican Church of Butembo with Pastor Ise-somo and church leaders outside. 18. Our house-to-be. 19. The site for Brett and Raya Newell's house – due to arrive March 1988. 20. The Primary School with 960 children. 21. Matt and Mike riding their bikes followed by some of the kids. 22. The school meeting hut – also used by the nightwatchman. 23. The roof held on with rocks. 24. Pastor Ise-somo's house and outside kitchen, with Mama Pastor pounding cassava.

HELPERS AND BOGHOLES
MAIL PLANES AND BREAD

We now had two workers. Wendy gave Annie her first instructions, and now it was my turn to begin teaching Ferdinand how to be our house helper. As the bathroom was still awash, I thought that he could start there. Wendy had bought a broom, mop and bucket in the market, and Ferdinand got to work.

Annie was on her way to the well down the hill. The well was not as we imagined. It was just a 40 cm square piece of wood over a hole in the ground. Using a five-litre plastic container (with the top cut off at a 45-degree angle) attached to a two-metre-long stick, Annie could reach the water and scoop up a litre or so and then repeat the procedure until the two 20-litre containers were full.

Ferdinand finished the bathroom and Wendy set him up to do the washing.

Annie finished ladling small amounts of water into the bidons making *five* trips to fill just *one* of the two 44-gallon drums. She was unable to fill the second drum as the water was becoming very muddy, so she asked for another task. Because Ferdinand was doing the washing in basins just outside the back door, we suggested she wash the floors. (This would have to be done every day with the amount of dirt and mud being traipsed through with the boys running in and out plus the visitors.)

We tried to communicate to her that Ferdinand had already washed the bathroom floor and that she could start in the corridor, so she washed the bathroom floor.

Wendy and I looked at each other, having totally failed to communicate our needs to this girl who probably didn't know French, as she hadn't been to high school, and our limited Swahili hadn't done the trick. We decided to cut our losses and have a coffee.

When it was time to fill the blue plastic 22-gallon drum which we used for drinking water, Annie had to walk the two kilometres to the 'source'. This was a water pipe set in a square concreted hole with steps leading down to the pipe. It was free to the community, having been constructed by an overseas AID organisation. To get this water she took only one bidon, waited her turn, filled it, balanced the now heavy container on her head and walked the two kilometres back. Full of water, the bidon weighs 20 kgs, but we realised she had been carrying water in containers since she was a small child and had built up the strength for those larger bidons. Still, it was quite a feat, and her posture was perfect.

We came to Butembo with the idea we would try *not* to have house help, but without basic things like water and electricity (which we take for granted in a developed country), we couldn't cope for a day! We were also helping the economy by providing jobs, and so we acquiesced.

The end of their day was meant to be 3pm. Wendy had to insist Ferdinand go home at 4.30pm but Annie didn't leave till 5.30. The reason? I was out with the boys and they didn't want Wendy left on her own. (That was a good sign, we thought.)

Gordon had turned up and asked if we wanted to go and see an impressive boghole. The four boys and I climbed aboard the Land Rover and drove through town heading north on the Beni road. We came to the boghole – it *was* impressive. You entered it via the two tyre-tracks you had no choice but to follow. The mud walls were higher than the Land Rover. Trucks would get bogged, the local villagers would dig them out for a fee, the hole got bigger, and the trucks kept getting bogged and the holes kept getting deeper and deeper. This was the main 'highway'. If there were a lot of trucks and you couldn't get past, you'd have to spend the night at the boghole *(as we did on the odd occasion – most memorably one New Year's Eve!)*. But for the transcontinental truck drivers they could be marooned in the mud for up to three weeks unable to squeeze past like we did in the Land Rover that day with Gordon. The challenges of travel in Zaïre.

We arrived home tired and ready for the dinner, bath and bed routine. By 11.15pm Wendy was sound asleep, but I was finishing some letters for the MAF plane, due in the following day, Wednesday. The plane would take these letters back to the MAF base at Nyankunde and then on to Bunia, the major town to the north, to connect with the MAF Kenya flight that came on Fridays. MAF Kenya would take the mail to Nairobi to be posted back to Australia. Quite simple really!

It wasn't long before people were asking when I would begin the dental work. 'When my equipment arrives,' was my standard answer. However, today the wife of a local businessman turned up at our house needing a simple extraction. I examined her sitting on a chair out in front of the house, surrounded by onlookers. Unfortunately, I couldn't do anything without instruments or equipment, but told her some basic instruments might be arriving with *wageni* (visitors) due the following Friday. If the instruments come, I might be able to do the extraction.

This sounds like a very simple interaction, but I couldn't understand what she was saying and had to call Brian Fagan to translate. Still, it was a fun experience for one who was keen to get working!

Just then Michael arrived home covered in dust, crying, with a grazed hip and elbow after taking an apparently spectacular fall off his bike. Everything had to be put on hold until we were able to clean him up and get some Band Aids on the wounds.

Matthew went off on his own to buy bread, to one of the local 'dukas' (those tiny roadside 'shops'). They sold him stale bread and charged him 50 zaïres for a half-size loaf of bread (normally only 20). He felt, like we all did, unable to communicate properly. I went back with him and requested the change, quietly but firmly. The lady told me the price was 30 zaïres. I went to the duka next door and asked their price. They told me it was 20. Once 'duka one' lady knew that I knew, she begrudgingly refunded all the money. But she wasn't bothered – she was just trying us out.

SHOCKS AND SURPRISES

It was early days, and we were still in the 'tourist stage'. Everything was new, different, and exciting. Well mostly.

The kids, constantly calling out *'Muzungu, muzungu'* ('white person, white person') at first was cute, but after several days with no let-up it started to wear thin. Everywhere we went we were surrounded by a swarm of kids.

We realised very quickly that we were going to need many trips to town to obtain what we needed just to survive. Basic household goods like cooking pots, cutlery and crockery, beds, sheets, towels and blankets. We had a whole lot of household things in 'those barrels' in the container that was coming from Australia, bringing the belongings for all the CMS families plus some building supplies and my dental equipment; but it wasn't due to arrive for several weeks – or perhaps months.

The shops in town were a challenge, as you never knew which one had the article you wanted. So, if you were after that very necessary commodity, toilet paper, you may have to visit a dozen shops which all look like they sell the same goods, only to be told 'sorry, no toilet paper, but we do have Nescafé and shower caps'.

One way around this, we discovered, was to hire 'runners'. There were many unemployed young men hanging round town, and when they saw someone looking for something, they'd come running to ask, 'What do you want? What do you need?' Then off they'd run to find the articles or supplies needed. They were especially keen if it was for a 'muzungu', as this meant they could hike up the price significantly with the shopkeeper and share the profits.

—

We had been given lectures at St Andrews Hall about culture shock and we had a sort of understanding of the three stages that people moving from one culture to another are going to experience. We knew about the 'tourist stage' for the first few weeks, we knew theoretically about the 'emotional dive' that happens as the reality of the new life, the new home, the new language, hits home and we knew theoretically that we would probably come out of it as our bodies adjusted to a new climate and our minds adjusted to our new circumstances.

However, when you are in it, you forget everything and just feel wretched. You are turned from a competent speaker in your country to a bumbling fool with the language skills of a three-year-old in your new location. And all the while, you have children peering in your curtain-less windows all day every day, until you can get some curtains or put up a fence.

There was a lot to get used to and a lot of simple little 'living' problems to solve before we even got to the problems of the older boys and schoolwork (when did that happen?) and then for me, when the container arrived, how would I go about setting up a dental clinic here?

—

My discouragement was not helped by our first experience of theft. It was such a small thing, but it really upset us.

It upset me.

It upset Wendy.

And it probably upset the kids too, because when the parents are upset it can spill over and affect the children.

You ask yourself, 'Why?'

'Why would someone steal it?'

You ask yourself, were we not vigilant enough?

SHOCKS AND SURPRISES

Were we too trusting?

Who could have taken it?

Who was around at the time?

How can we get another one to replace it here in the middle of nowhere?

We have so few 'things' we agonised, and someone has gone and stolen one of them.

'What were we going to do without it?'

We searched high and low.

We searched inside the house and in the outside kitchen.

We checked the swept dirt around the house and the grass on the verge.

We looked at the suspects.

Was it Annie, the girl who carries the water?

She has a need for it.

Did she take it?

Was it Ferdinand who does the washing?

He needs it, and his wife would love one.

Could he have taken it?

Was it the zamu?

He had shifty eyes, I thought.

Annie solved the problem, as she prepared to go to the distant water source with the yellow plastic 20-litre water container.

If the red plastic cap for the container has gone, you just stick a banana in the hole.

We never did find the culprit ... and ... we got over it.

But in that second week, on Wendy's birthday *(Happy Birthday Wendy and welcome to your new life)*; what do you do when someone steals the kerosene stove that you have put outside because of the fumes when you blow out the flame? It was no wonder that culture shock and culture fatigue began to hit us hard. (It did get better as we established routines and the strange became the familiar, but we were still missing home for some time.)

So it was a delight to welcome four Aussie visitors in those early weeks. As the MAF Cessna 206 circled the airstrip and then landed, I found I had tears in my eyes. Having friends from home visit was an emotional experience for both Wendy and me. Lloyd Bennett, a friend and fellow trumpet player in the CMS Summer School orchestra and his wife Isabel, daughter Cathy and a friend, arrived on Friday the 8th of January 1988. They came bearing gifts, including lots of books for the boys.

It was both a good thing and a bad thing having visitors from home so soon after our arrival. To see fellow Australians, people who speak the same language and have the same cultural background, was wonderful and we spent five very happy days with them. There was lots of Aussie talk about sports and politics and mutual friends. The kids loved having some young adults to hang out and play rough-and-tumble games with. The service to welcome them was longer than any we had experienced so far *(but not as long as some in the years to come)*.

On Sunday afternoon we took the opportunity to do the tourist thing and show our guests the latest boghole full of trucks. They too were suitably impressed.

Tuesday 12th of January was Lloyd and Isabel's 25th wedding anniversary and we celebrated by killing a goat. There is no finer place to celebrate a major life event than in Zaïre with goat meat. The kids watched the slaughter, both horrified and fascinated. I took a raincheck on that experience. Wendy was too busy to even contemplate it.

Visitors come and then they go. It was a wonderful diversion while they were there. But it was sad to watch the plane taking them away. Back to life the way we knew it. It took us a while to focus again.

The very next day our 'zamu' (night watchman) turned up for work drunk. We asked Ise-somo to come and help with translation. It seems the zamu's six-year-old had died the night before, his second child to die. Life is very sad here. Pastor prayed and then the zamu went back home. The child's body would be laid in the small 'salon' of the mud house. Family and friends would come and sit all through the night around the body, singing hymns and praying, usually the women inside and the men outside. And then the next day, when the rough-hewn coffin is made and the body prepared, they would all follow the coffin to the burial site. The zamu would return in a day or two, but the visitors would continue coming to pay their respects for days, even weeks. He would need help with funds to be able to feed all the visitors. So for tonight we would be without a night watchman. Death is common here. Sadness visits often and we were affected too.

———

But things change rapidly and for our kids the next day was a day of delight. The Lodens delivered us a pup from their litter and the boys immediately called the dog Rusty.

While they were off playing with their new best friend, a red Land Rover could be seen on the track on the next hill heading our way.

Could this be the Service Médicale vehicle we had been promised?

It stopped and out stepped a very thin but dignified-looking young Zairian woman who introduced herself as Nyangoma. She was the Service Médicale supervisor from Boga and, hallelujah, this was the Butembo medical vehicle! Her driver was introduced as Telesphor, or Tele for short. We greeted him and shook hands in the African fashion, with a swivel. We were going to spend a lot of time with Tele in the future. He was present the day of the shooting that I never wrote home about. But that story is for another day or another book.

The next day Nyangoma and I went on safari to Mumole (pronounced 'Moo-mo-lay'). The vehicle started off with 18 people inside but to my surprise, 11 got off in the city of Butembo, three kilometres from home. *(They were just hitching a ride to town!)* We drove 40 kms into the North Kivu hills on the muddy and potholed track masquerading as a road, and stopped to visit two health centres, Kilau and Mumole. Nyangoma informed one of the nurses at Mumole that she was being transferred back to Boga, the centre of the Anglican health work. She had 20 minutes to pack her things and then she was off in the Land Rover with us. The reason? Two nurses had died in Boga. One had drowned in the Semliki River and the other died in a car accident.

While I was away for the day, Wendy had an afternoon caller. Cathy Loden had dropped in to visit in the morning and had given us a plate laden with freshly baked cookies – a real treat, and the plan was to ration them out over several days.

But Wendy made a mistake.

Unaware of local custom, she put out the plate that Cathy had brought with all the cookies on it. The 'afternoon caller' had a cup of tea with Wendy and shared a cookie or two while they made stilted conversation in Swahili. But Wendy was gobsmacked when she came to leave. She lifted the plate with all the remaining cookies and dropped them into her basket, bade farewell in Swahili and departed. Wendy was left with nothing but an open mouth, and an empty plate.

It was late January 1988. In Australia everyone was preparing for the Bicentennial Celebrations, but we were totally cut off – our only form of communication were the letters that arrived four to six weeks after they were posted. We did however have our own small bicentennial celebration. Wendy made a cake in the shape of Australia and our Canadian friends happened to call in as we were celebrating and joined us in singing the Australian National Anthem (without knowing the words – it's the thought that counts).

We had plenty to keep ourselves busy, the boys were enjoying the adventure of being in Zaïre, we were getting to know our new surroundings, along with some of the local people and we were appreciating the help Pastor Ise-somo was giving us almost every day.

We had arrived.

The long road to Zaïre was over and we had found our home for the next few years.

We didn't realise that getting here was the easy part.

ACKNOWLEDGEMENTS AND REFLECTION

This manuscript was finally finished, on our youngest son's birthday, close to Christmas 2021. It first began more than ten years ago, so many rough drafts, so many attempts. It dribbled on until 2017 when prostate cancer, successfully treated with surgery, made me realise that if I was ever going to finish this book, I'd better get cracking.

It is impossible to thank everyone who has played a part in the process of writing this book without forgetting someone. But you have, each in your own way, encouraged me to continue and I am thankful for that.

Did I answer the question from our adult children that I put at the start of this book?

'Dad and Mum, what were you thinking?'

It's very hard to know. I have told you the story as it unfolded as best I can, with Wendy's help. Did God call us with an audible voice? No, not at all. What then? How do you explain what you did? I can't. But something happened that year at CMS Summer School that touched both Wendy's heart and mine when we heard about the need in Zaïre. Why not Tanzania or Uzbekistan? I have no idea but our response, I guess deep down, was based on Christian concern to use our gifts to help people and the challenge of the verse – 'If anyone has the world's goods and sees his brother in need, yet closes his heart against him, how does God's love abide in him?' (1 John 3:17)

Mum, Neal (13) me and Dad (1949)

Mum, me, and Dad – Debutante Ball (1954)

Me and Rosalyn (1955)

Me (aged 16) in Wollongong Steelworks Band uniform with Junior State Championship Trophy

Wollongong High School Jazz Band (1964)

Me, Rosalyn, Mum and Dad (1969)

Manma and Pop's 60th Wedding Anniversary

Wendy and me on our Wedding Day (May 1973)

Wendy and me with Rev Peter Boase

With Wendy's parents, Dorothy and John Stirling

Loading the bus in Kathmandu, Nepal (February 1976)

Landslide on the road from Srinagar, Kashmir

Me, Wendy, Mike and Deb camping in Baghdad, Iraq

John Stott and Frances Whitehead with Wendy at the Hookses in Wales – John was working on the manuscript for his Ephesians Commentary (1978)

Bill and Robyn Hawkshaw, Noël Tredinnick, Wendy, Fiona Tredinnick, Pam (surname unknown) and Michael Baughen – Katoomba (1980)

Mike, Wendy, Steve, Jem, me and Matthew (1986)

Dr Paul White speaking at our Valedictory Service (1987)

MAF at Butembo airstrip

Hills surrounding Butembo

Patients outside Mumole village clinic (1988)

www.ingramcontent.com/pod-product-compliance
Lightning Source LLC
Chambersburg PA
CBHW060503090426
42735CB00011B/2094